The Business Strategy Audit

A Company Self-Appraisal to Analyze the Effectiveness of Your Business Strategy and Your Strategy-Making Process

Vernal Della-Piana, Murray Low & Kendall Lyman

Novations Group Inc

FINANCIAL TIMES
Prentice Hall

An imprint of **PEARSON EDUCATION**

London · New York · San Francisco · Toronto · Sydney
Tokyo · Singapore · Hong Kong · Cape Town · Madrid · Paris · Milan · Munich · Amsterdam

PEARSON EDUCATION LIMITED

Head Office:
Edinburgh Gate
Harlow CM20 2JE
Tel: +44 (0)1279 623623
Fax: +44 (0)1279 431059

London Office:
128 Long Acre, London WC2E 9AN
Tel: +44 (0)207 447 2000
Fax: +44 (0)207 240 5771
Website: www.business-minds.com

First published in Great Britain in 2000

© Cambridge Strategy Publications Ltd 2000

Published in association with
Cambridge Strategy Publication Ltd
39 Cambridge Place
Cambridge CB2 1NS

The right of Vernal Della-Piana, Murray Low and Kendall Lyman to be
identified as Authors of this Work has been asserted by them in accordance
with the Copyright, Design and Patents Act 1988.

ISBN 0 273 64709 1

British Library Cataloguing in Publication Data
A CIP catalogue record for this book can be obtained from the British Library

10 9 8 7 6 5 4 3 2

Typeset by Pantek Arts, Maidstone, Kent
Printed and bound in Great Britain

The Publishers' policy is to use paper manufactured from sustainable forests.

CONTENTS

INTRODUCTION

Nearly all of the major initiatives undertaken by corporate executives today are called "strategic." With everything having high strategic importance, it is becoming increasingly difficult to distinguish between the many priorities and imperatives that are initiated in organizations. *When everything is clearly strategic, often nothing strategic is clear.* When everything is designated as a high priority, there are, in reality, no priorities at all.

When strategic direction is clearly understood by everyone throughout an organization, the following benefits occur:

- organizational capabilities are aligned to support the achievement of strategy,

- resources are allocated in priority order according to a process' contribution to competitive advantage, and

- a company can excel in the market place.

The purpose of the strategy audit is to arm managers with the tools, information, and commitment to evaluate the degree of advantage and focus provided by their current strategies. The audit produces the data needed to determine whether a change in strategy is needed and what any necessary changes should be. It should be understood that once the strategy audit process is begun, it is difficult to return to where the organization started because executives will be inclined to change the strategy, and employees will have gained energy for change.

A Word about Strategy

Strategy, in its proper form, should provide managers with a framework for decision making and resource allocation that will lead to clarity of purpose and to the achievement of competitive advantage. Corporate leaders not interested in leading their industry should avoid the seduction of paying attention to strategy. Strategy should not be developed because its the "right" thing to do. *Without the drive to win, there is no reason for an organization to suffer the upheaval and work involved in strategy clarification, of which the audit is the first step.*

Defining the Strategy Audit

The strategy audit involves assessing the actual direction of a business and comparing that course to the direction required to succeed in a changing environment. A company's actual direction is the sum of what it does and does not do, how well the organization is internally aligned to support the strategy, and how viable the strategy is when compared to external market, competitor and financial realities. These two categories, the internal assessment and the external or environmental assessment, make up the major elements of the audit format presented in the pages that follow. In the final analysis, the strategy audit results in an action plan that will make an organization's refined strategy more internally and externally robust.

This audit provides the following tools:

- A clear case for why managers should conduct a strategy audit.

- The tools, skills, language, information and frameworks necessary to conduct an audit.

- An understanding of how to collect the necessary information.

- Direction on how to analyze and understand the information gathered.

- A feeling that engaging in an audit process is really worthwhile.

- A description of why a strategy audit should be a highly participative process involving a cross-section of people from throughout the organization.

- A clear understanding of the implications of doing the audit.

- A list of the common mistakes made in performing strategy audits.

The guide is divided into five primary sections:

- Conducting an environmental assessment.

- Conducting an organizational assessment.

- Integrating and implementing the findings from the two assessments.

- The audit process.

- Questions and checklists to help plan and implement the audit.

Part 1

THE EXTERNAL ENVIRONMENT ASSESSMENT

The purpose of being in business is to provide distinct products and services to customers at a value superior to that offered by competitors. Without a strategy, valuable resources will be diluted, the work of employees will be unfocused, and distinctiveness will not be achieved. The external environment assessment provides a business with a critical external link between its competitors, customers, and the products/services it offers.

The environment is where distinctiveness is created and also where it is eliminated. The creation of distinctiveness occurs when a company identifies needs that exist in the environment and packages its products or services to meet customer needs in a way that is superior to the offerings of its competitors. Distinctiveness may also be created by introducing new products and services to meet needs that customers did not know existed. Customer needs may disappear because customers change or because another competitor finds a better way to meet those needs. As a result, the fundamental purpose for examining an organization's environment in the process of clarifying strategy can be summarized by the following three reasons:

• Ensure that the company is meeting the needs evident in the environment.

• Prevent others from meeting the needs in a better way.

• Create or identify ways to meet future or emerging needs.

The success or failure of a company often depends on its ability to monitor changes in the environment and meet the needs of its customers and prospective customers.

An organization's business environment is never static. What is viewed as uniqueness or distinctiveness today will be viewed as commonplace tomorrow as new competitors enter the industry or change the environment by modifying the rules by which companies compete. Consequently, an effective strategy will do more than help a company to stay in the game. Rather, it will help it to establish new rules for the game that favor that company. Successful companies do more than simply understand their environments. They also influence and shape the circumstances around them. Companies that fail to influence their environments automatically forfeit that right to their competitors.

Importance of External Environment Assessments

Every business already understands its business environment at a certain level. In most companies, those involved in the marketing and strategic planning areas routinely monitor the company's environment. Most people in these functions make consistent efforts to improve their analysis. The environmental assessment will help improve analysis by providing confirmation that this study of the environment is carried out rigorously and objectively, and will ensure that external analysis is geared toward achieving the company's strategy.

In too many cases, market research and strategic planning can become ends in and of themselves, rather than a means to making good strategic decisions. This happens when planning and marketing activities become focused on internal issues and measures instead of focusing on the larger business environment. Many companies reward people who perform a specific function well, and have greater difficulty rewarding those whose scope extends beyond organizational boundaries. Therefore, the vision of routine external analysis is often limited. The tendency to focus inward is influenced by the day-to-day demands of working within a company. The complexity of managing any single part of the business well consumes the energy and attention that might otherwise be used to step back and look at the broader picture.

An inward focus can also be a by-product of a company's success. A business that dominates its industry may no longer feel the need to be rigorous in understanding what it does that has made it so successful. Managers become focused inward on how to manage success, rather than continuing to find new ways to generate success by maintaining a broad vision.

An inward focus will eventually lead to a company's demise as environments change. Sometimes changes in the environment are significant and obvious. New factors develop that are widely known and understood, as when new chips are introduced into the computer industry. At other times, changes are discreet and subtle, occurring over time and understood only in hindsight. US automobile industry leaders can attest to the impact on their industry of Japanese competitors' superior performance. This impact is no less significant than the dramatic developments that have occurred in other industries, even though increased competition did not develop suddenly. Paying attention to the environment ensures that a company is prepared for change rather than being blind-sided by it.

In summary, the environmental assessment provides a context for a company to understand its purpose. It answers two fundamental questions: Who is winning and why? and What must we do to survive? It provides insight into what a company must do to gain competitive advantage. It also reminds the internal organization that it exists to serve an external need. This understanding is critical to the survival and success of the organization.

STEPS IN CONDUCTING AN EXTERNAL ENVIRONMENT ASSESSMENT

The conceptual framework that is used in this section illustrates three main industry components:

• Direct providers of goods or services (producers — for both the company and its competitors).

• Direct users of goods or services (customers).

• Indirect influencers on customers and producers (stakeholders).

Each of these components needs to be understood from two perspectives: where it is today, and the forces that will change its direction in the future. The goal of an environmental assessment is to develop a better understanding within the company of these issues and their application. In order for a company to lead an industry, people in the organization must understand these issues better than their competitors do. The methodology to accomplish this includes three steps:

Step 1: Understand the Environment at a Macro Level

Step 2: Understand the Industry Components in Detail

Step 3: Integrate the Components into an Environmental Picture

Who Should Conduct the Assessment?

We have found that the steps above are best accomplished through study teams. Four teams or analysis groups are needed to conduct the environmental assessment. A leadership team has the task of overseeing the entire process; it should complete the first and third steps. Three separate study teams should be organized to look at the issues in greater detail as part of the second step. The study process is described visually in Figure 1.

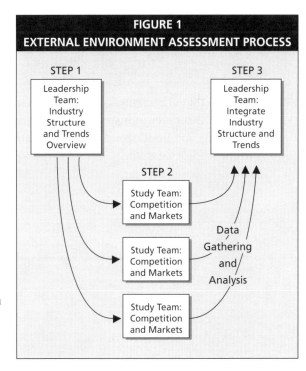

FIGURE 1

EXTERNAL ENVIRONMENT ASSESSMENT PROCESS

STEP 1

Leadership Team: Industry Structure and Trends Overview

STEP 3

Leadership Team: Integrate Industry Structure and Trends

STEP 2

Study Team: Competition and Markets

Study Team: Competition and Markets

Study Team: Competition and Markets

Data Gathering and Analysis

UNDERSTAND THE EXTERNAL ENVIRONMENT AT A MACRO LEVEL

The first step in the environmental assessment is to develop a basic understanding of the trends and issues that will significantly change, influence, and affect the industry. This step includes fundamental questions about the nature of the industry: who, what, where, when, why, and how companies do things. It looks at the economic returns that the industry generates and how capital markets react to those returns. In addition, this step addresses what is needed to compete and win in the industry, and how those factors are changing.

Broad industry changes occur much more slowly than changes in individual players or markets within the industry. Industries merge (telecommunications, cable television and computers) create spin-offs (PC from mainframes) and even die (telegraph). The ideal level of analysis in the industry overview is to understand the broader shifts that go beyond specific markets. For example, the telecommunications industry is composed of sub industries: service providers, equipment providers, etc. Within each sub-industry there are several markets. For service providers, sub-industries include long distance, regional, local, etc. For equipment providers, there are suppliers to end users, resellers, etc. Each of these markets can be broken into smaller segments that are essential to business strategy. The industry overview should not be concerned with detailed market segmentation, as this will be considered in the detailed analysis. Instead, the focus in Step 1 is on the broader trends across and within industries, including smaller industries and broader markets.

The overall industry understanding comes from looking at the elements that influence the environment. These elements include the following:

- Capital markets

- Industry capacity

- Technological factors

- Pressure from substitutes

- Threat of new entrants

- Economic factors

- Political factors

- Regulatory factors

- Geographic factors

- Social factors.

Team Staffing

The leadership team should be made up of representative managers or leaders of different functions or groups within the company. Additional people might be added to the team to ensure a wide range of backgrounds, talents, and interests. The inclusion of key technical players, "natural" leaders, and idea leaders from within the organization enhances the team's ability to look at the broad environmental picture presented by these elements.

The natural tendency of leadership teams performing an environmental overview is to undertake a superficial analysis. In most companies, upper management team members have very informed viewpoints about the issues in this analysis. However, they inevitably neglect certain aspects of the environment, focusing their efforts on managing and running a business from day to day.

This fact requires that three critical elements be considered in conducting the overview. The first is that the environmental assessment must be conducted from an external perspective. Second, the assessment needs to be conducted with rigor and be based on data, rather than being based on intuitive insight. Finally, managers have a tendency to disregard negative information about the company and its products. The leadership team must be honest and open about what is really happening in the environment.

Information sources usually available for this part of the audit are listed in Figure 2. The nature of the industry and the leadership team's access to the sources will dictate how much each source should be used.

Some sources are more important for some industries than others. For example, technology is a much more critical factor in the computer industry than it is in the timber industry. Therefore, a company in the computer industry would require an extensive review of the technological issues by interviewing industry experts and

---

FIGURE 2
INFORMATION SOURCES

PRINT SOURCES:
- Business and industry periodicals
- World Bank studies
- Industry reports
- Consulting analysts' reports
- Investment analysts' reports
- Trade publications
- Government agency reports
- Trade association reports

INTERVIEW SOURCES:
- Investment bankers
- Industry analysts
- Technical experts
- Consultants
- Industry association leaders
- Government leaders
- Former CEO/industry leaders

OTHER:
- Computer information services
- Computer-generated reports

reading relevant articles from technology journals. The data sources shown in Figure 2 are usually also sufficient for the specific industry research that follows the general industry assessment.

After reviewing the type of information needed and the suggested information sources, the leadership team should decide how to gather the information. A useful framework to understand these issues comes from answering the questions suggested in Figure 3. These questions are posed directly when used in the context of an interview, and used indirectly when analyzing data.

Answering these questions from various perspectives (economic, technological, political, geographical, etc.) provides an initial viewpoint about the direction of the industry. The analysis will also identify areas requiring further study. These can be explored by the industry component study teams in Step Two, who will share their findings with the leadership team.

FIGURE 3
INDUSTRY QUESTIONS

- What is the long-term viability of the industry as a whole, and how do capital markets react to new developments?
- What trends could change the rules of the game?
- Who are the industry leaders? What are they doing? Why?
- What are the key success factors in the industry?
- What developments could allow a company to change the rules of the game?
- Five years from now, how will winners in the industry look and act?
- What is the reward (and/or cost) of being a winner/loser within the industry?
- Where has the industry come from?

UNDERSTAND THE INDUSTRY COMPONENTS IN DETAIL

This section deals with the future and long-term viability of the industry in greater detail. It focuses on the same three industry components:

• The company and its competitors

• Customers

• Other stakeholders

The teams that study these components should understand the elements of both the overall strategy audit and the environmental assessment that their analysis will contribute to. Preliminary findings and identification of important issues from the leadership team's review of the overall environment are the prerequisites for the study teams to begin their work.

Team Tasks

Each team studying the components of the environment has two fundamental tasks. The first is to use the industry analysis questions from Figure 3 to analyze where each group sees the industry heading. For example, the customer group would seek to understand the customers' perceptions of industry trends, success factors, changes, etc. The questions from Figure 3 provide a framework for interviewing customers, competitors and stakeholders about the environment.

The second task is to address specific issues that are significant about the particular part of the industry assigned to a given study team. The research of each of these teams should be analyzed at the same level, and should use the same framework for industry segmentation.

This section of the audit suggests questions that should be answered for each of the industry components. Three areas will be addressed:

• What information is needed?

• How is the information obtained and from whom?

• How should the information be analyzed?

FIGURE 4
RESEARCH QUESTIONS

A. BUSINESS REVIEW

Strategy Issues:
- What is the strategy of each competitor? Where do they appear to be heading?
- What is their business emphasis?
- Do they compete on quality, cost, speed or service?
- Are they niche or global players?

Capabilities:
- What do they do better than anyone else?
- Where are they weaker than others?
- Where are they the same as others?

Business Objectives:
- Who are their primary customers?
- What types of business do they not do or say no to?
- Who are their major partners? Why are they partnering? What do they gain by partnering?
- What are they doing that is new or interesting?

B. FINANCIAL REVIEW

Financial Strength — Internal:
- How much cash does each competitor generate annually?
- What are the drivers behind their financial success (from a cash perspective)?
- How do they allocate resources (funds)?
- How fast are they growing and in what areas?

Strength as Perceived by Capital Markets:
- Are competitors resource constrained or do they have strong financial backing?
- Is this perception consistent with the internal analysis? Why or why not?
- How has the company performed in the financial markets? Why?
- What constraints/opportunities do they have with respect to financial markets? Why?

C. ORGANIZATION REVIEW

Top Management:
- Has management kept the company at the forefront of the industry? Why or why not?
- Are the key players seen to be moving the company forward?

Organization:
- Is the company centralized or decentralized?
- Does the corporate parent act as a holding company or as an active manager?
- Is the organization perceived as being lean and able to get things done?

People:
- How many people are employed? Is the company over- or under- staffed?
- Are people managed to achieve mainly business objectives, human objectives or some of both? How does this affect the company?
- What skills are emphasized during recruitment?

Culture:
- Is the culture results-oriented?
- Bureaucratic?
- Flexible?

The study teams for competitors and customers will use these questions to a greater extent than will the stakeholder team.

1. COMPETITION AND MARKETS

The purpose of studying competitors in the industry is to understand how they intend to create or maintain competitive advantage in comparison to other players in the industry. The two components of advantage are current distinctiveness, and positioning for future distinctiveness. Current distinctiveness is determined by assessing a competitor's current strength and position in the marketplace. Positioning for future distinctiveness stems from the capabilities a company has today that will enable it to excel in the future.

What information is needed?

The information to be gathered about competitors falls under three main categories: business, financial and organization. The questions to be answered under each section are outlined in Figure 4.

How is the information obtained and from whom?

Obtaining the information for this part of the analysis is difficult since competitors are not in the practice of volunteering information to each other. However, much of the information is publicly available from annual reports, investment presentations, journal articles, financial reports and reviews (internal and external), interviews with customers, interviews with industry analysts/experts, interviews with former employees of competitors, and other published information.

Interview information is the most sensitive part of data gathering. Customers, industry experts, and other external sources often feel uncomfortable talking about other companies. Two things can be done to improve the quality of the information gathered: 1) do up front analysis on the available public data to identify key areas of focus, and 2) ask questions in a way that does not require the person being interviewed to compromise his or her integrity. For example, interviewers need not gather specific information about each of the company's competitors. General questions such as "Which companies are the industry leaders and why?" or "Who is doing better or worse than expected and why?" draw out specific information about competitors. If a competitor has a particular strength, then the interviewer might ask something like, "Why do you think Company X does this better than anyone else?"

How should the information be analyzed?

The purpose of gathering the information outlined above is to understand what distinguishes industry leaders from industry followers. It should provide clues as to

FIGURE 5
COMPETITOR ANALYSIS

	Competitor A	Competitor B	Competitor C	Competitor D
Business	+	=	=	=
Financial	-	+	-	=
Organization	=	=	-	+

+ Has competitive advantage
= At parity with competitors
- At competitive disadvantage

who is doing better or worse than expected and why this performance gap exists. It is helpful to organize the information into two matrices: one that reflects the current position of competitors and one that projects their future positioning. Figure 5 shows how this can be done:

One of the goals of this matrix is to determine whether any one competitor has a clear competitive advantage in the industry. It is also useful to compare the company conducting the audit to others in the industry using this framework. This provides an early indication of whether or not the company's processes support, or are aligned with, its strategy.

2. CUSTOMERS

The purpose of studying customers is to understand the interface and relationship a company has with those who buy its products and services. Managers should understand where the company does business in the industry, which includes knowing who its customers are, what products they buy, and why those customers choose to do business with the company rather than with its competitors. More importantly, managers need to understand the factors that will influence where customers will do business in the future.

What information is needed?

Two general types of analysis are needed with respect to customers (in addition to the general industry perceptions previously noted): an understanding of how customers affect the company, and an understanding of how the company affects the customer and the customers' business. This understanding should be framed both in terms of where the company is today, and where it is likely to be in the future.

Understanding the Customers' Impact on the Company

This is an internal analysis that addresses this fundamental question: What does the company gain from working with a particular customer? It is conducted from both a market or financial perspective and a strategic or business perspective. The analysis from each perspective is fundamentally different.

The *financial or market analysis* seeks to clarify the effect a customer has on the profitability of the company. All major customers should be assessed in terms of:

• Sales and sales growth trends.

• Gross margin on products sold.

• Other costs required to do business with the customer (cost to serve).

This last point is particularly important as most accounting systems lump the overhead associated with serving customers into functional overhead categories. The other costs typically included in this category are sales costs, delivery costs, customer service costs and administrative costs (order entry, invoicing, collections, etc.).

The *business or strategic perspective* seeks to clarify what the company does for the customer. It seeks to measure the intangible costs and benefits of doing business with them, as well as assessing the company's understanding of how well it knows its customers' needs. This perspective will be revisited after gathering data from the customers' perspective. The questions to ask include the following:

• Does the business we do with this customer provide us with competitive advantage that is transferable to other customers?

• What resources are we giving up by working with this customer that we could use to service other customers?

• Why do we think the customer buys from us? What do we provide for them that others do not provide?

Again, these questions are asked both in terms of where the company is today and where managers see the business going.

Understanding the Company's Impact on the Customer or Customer's Business

Understanding the company's impact on the customer requires a different approach depending on whether the customer is another business or an individual consumer. The analysis for each of the two scenarios is similar in many respects, but there are subtle differences. The commercial customer will be discussed first, followed by the process for the consumer.

Commercial Customers

Understanding the company's impact on the customer's business is the most basic element of business strategy. Many companies lose sight of this as their raison d'être. Most companies place a high value on customer insight and knowledge, whether they do so intuitively or by design. Managers know that without this understanding, the company will become too internally focused, take its eye off the ball, and allow someone else to take away what they have developed.

The purpose of this part of the analysis is to help the audit team understand the customer's business better than competitors and potential competitors understand it. The frameworks used for doing the industry study and the competitive analysis can be modified and used in the customer analysis. Three critical areas should be addressed to understand the customer:

• Understand the customer's environment (or industry) at a macro level.

• Understand the customer's business and place in the industry in detail.

• Understand how the company fits into what the customer does and what part it plays in determining where the customer is in the industry today, and where it is heading in the industry.

This analysis should clarify how what the company does contributes to the competitive advantage of its customers and makes them successful. This analysis is based on the assumption that understanding a customer's strategy and contributing to its achievement assures a long term relationship with the customer.

Understanding a customer's environment and industry includes investigating the same topics that were covered in the macro-level assessment for the company. While this analysis can be completed in less detail, it should still include an analysis of the key industry influences. These include capital markets, capacity, substitutes, technology, economics, etc. Then the impact of industry developments on the industry and the customer should be assessed.

The broad industry assessment is followed by a more detailed assessment of the customers' business. The information and data necessary to complete the analysis falls under the same three categories as it did for the competitor analysis: business, financial and organization. The detailed questions from the competitor section (Figure 5) are also relevant to understanding customers and their direction.

The final step in understanding commercial customers involves exploring how the company fits into the customer's business, its industry and where it is heading. This analysis should be done at three levels within the organization: at a broad strategic level, at an operational level, and at an ease-of-doing-business level.

The strategic level. The analysis at the strategic level involves determining how the company adds value to its customer's business from an economic and strategic perspective. This requires an understanding of how the company contributes to the customer's competitive advantage. A key indicator of this is the customer's perception of the company's strengths and weaknesses in relation to competitors.

The operational level. Understanding the operational level interface requires a detailed understanding of why customers buy from the company rather than from its competitors. This is done by looking at the buyer-purchase criteria, a general viewpoint about which is gained from the strategic or broad interface. Buyer-purchase criteria analysis is done by answering the following questions:

• Why do customers buy from us instead of from others?

• What factors influence buying decisions and what is the relative importance of these factors?

• What do customers look at when comparing products?

• Who usually gets the sale? Why?

The purpose of doing buyer-purchase criteria analysis is to understand the most important buying factors from the customer's perspective. In general, these factors include product features such as cost, quality, service, or innovation.

The ease-of-doing-business level. The ease-of-doing-business issues include an understanding of the factors of doing business with the company. These include simple issues such as billing, customer service, order processing, communications, etc. The purpose of looking at these factors is to assess whether the company is attending to them in such a way that it does not create competitive disadvantage.

Individual Consumers

The analysis for customers who are individual consumers is more simple than that for businesses. In-depth market analysis will provide the necessary information for understanding the customer. A review of trends, demographics, customer preferences, buying patterns, social factors, etc. gives insight into how the company's products affect the customer. This analysis includes the buyer-purchase criteria discussed above and goes still further by looking at the broader shifts in consumer tastes. Much of this research may have been done by the market research staff, or it may be available commercially.

How is the information obtained and from whom?

The customer analysis needs to include a broad sampling of customers for different products. There are generally one or two lead customers or customer groups responsible for the majority of sales for each product. These customers must be included in the analysis. It is also important to talk to different types of customers: new customers, customers in different industries, customers who put the product to different end uses, etc. Past customers who have recently switched to another supplier are a prime information source.

The best source of information varies for each segment of the customer analysis:

Impact on the Business:

- Financial — cost data from accounting and marketing analysis.

- Strategic — interviews with internal company executives, marketing staff, sales staff and others who have frequent customer contact, annual reports, and data from public sources.

Impact on the Customer's Business:

Commercial Customer

- Environment — industry publications, interviews with industry analysts and top company executives.

- Business strategy — interviews with a broad cross section of customer company executives.

- How the company fits in — interviews with people within the customer business who make purchasing decisions or who interface with the company on a regular basis.

Individual Consumers

- Market analyst reports, consumer interviews and focus groups, demographic and social trends.

How should the information be analyzed?

The purpose of gathering customer data is to ensure that the company is meeting customer needs today, and that it will continue to do so in the future. Customers collectively provide a mirror on the organization's strengths and weaknesses in the marketplace. Gaps in perceptions between what the customers think and the company's view of itself are inevitable. In addition, customers may also confirm some aspects of the company's view of itself. Customers reinforce these beliefs and often add significant insight into the roots of company strengths and weaknesses.

The data gathered from and about customers should be examined along three dimensions:

1) Today and the future.

2) Importance to the company and importance to the customer.

3) From the customer's perspective and from the company's perspective.

The fundamental question that needs to be addressed within these dimensions is to identify how the company does or does not create distinctiveness with the customer and why this is so.

3. STAKEHOLDERS

The purpose of conducting stakeholder analysis is to understand the indirect influences on the industry and the company. Stakeholders include those beyond a company's customers and competitors who affect or are affected by the company and its operations. They may include suppliers, regulatory agencies, public interest groups, stock holders, etc. Stakeholder analysis is broader and less detailed than customer or competitor analysis. The analysis is similar to the overall environmental analysis, but is conducted in greater depth and with more rigor.

What information is needed?

The analysis is designed to determine the expectations and viewpoints of stakeholders with respect to the company. The questions that need to be asked of stakeholders include the following:

• What does the stakeholder need from the company?

• What does the stakeholder value about the company?

• What is the stakeholder's role in relation to the business?

• What do they expect of the company?

• What are some potential roadblocks for the company as it pursues its business objectives?

- What opportunities should the company pursue that differ from what it is doing today?

- Does the stakeholder have a viewpoint about what the company can do to achieve competitive advantage in the marketplace?

The viewpoints expressed by stakeholders often differ substantially from what customers say or what industry analysts foresee. Stakeholders have their own objectives; the company's activities affect the achievement of those objectives. Stakeholders typically express their opinions without regard to the company's business purpose, even though what they do and think will influence that purpose.

How is the information obtained and from whom?

The stakeholders that a company needs to understand include the following groups:

- Shareholders

- End users

- Environmental groups

- Politicians/public policy experts

- Regulatory agencies

- Joint venture partners

- Technologists

- Corporate holding company

Interviews can be conducted with representatives from each of the stakeholder groups, and also with others who understand the perspectives of various stakeholders.

How should the information be analyzed?

Interview responses from stakeholders should be grouped into three categories: expectations, opportunities and threats. Most of the stakeholders will be very supportive of company activities because they have clear expectations that are aligned with what the company is trying to achieve. However, a few stakeholders will point out threats and constraints that the company needs to consider as it moves forward.

INTEGRATE THE COMPONENTS INTO AN ENVIRONMENTAL PICTURE

Once the study teams have reported their findings on the stakeholder analysis, customer analysis and competitor analysis, leadership team members should step back and integrate the data. Integrating the different components will help the team to understand the overall environment in which the business operates. This integration should take place at two levels: assessing where the industry is heading and the likely impact of that direction on the company, and combining the organizational assessment with the environmental assessment.

The information gathered can be analyzed using a framework similar to the one shown in Figure 6. The analysis highlights significant changes in the environment, and the impact of those changes on the company's competitive position within the industry. It addresses the fundamental question of how the company can influence its environment in the future, and what the business will need to look like if it is to thrive in the future. In addition, the analysis will highlight the requirements and capabilities that are needed within the company to meet external demands. These requirements and needs should then be matched up with the current capabilities outlined in the organization assessment. This will enable the team to determine the overall alignment of the company's strategy to its environment.

FIGURE 6 INDUSTRY ANALYSIS		
INDUSTRY COMPONENT	FINDINGS	IMPACT ON COMPANY
What is the viability of the industry?		
What developments could change the rules of the game?		
What are the industry leaders doing? Why?		
What are the key success factors in the industry?		
What will winners look like five years from now?		
Where is the industry heading?		
Which competitors are positioning themselves for industry leadership in the future? What capabilities do they have?		
What do customers want in the future?		

Part 2

THE
ORGANIZATIONAL
ASSESSMENT

Once the company's environment has been examined and analyzed, managers should consider the qualities and characteristics of the organization itself that influence what can be accomplished in terms of strategy. This section is about organizational assessment. The steps shown here will provide insights into the effectiveness of the company's current strategy, and provide guidelines for increasing strategic effectiveness.

The following elements are the components of understanding an organization from a strategic perspective.

- *Strategy Clarification.* Strategy clarification helps the leadership team determine what business they are in, the direction of the business, and framework or criteria for making strategic decisions in the future. If people at any level of a business are unclear about any of these three areas, it is difficult for them to focus their attention, cooperate with other teams, and organize their efforts to gain competitive advantage in the marketplace

- *Viability and Robustness.* Measuring viability and robustness helps a leadership team test strategies and ideas against future world scenarios to determine whether the strategies can be achieved and sustained. By looking at both market and financial viability and robustness in different scenarios, a management team can see what will create advantage in the future and what key measures need to be implemented to monitor changes in business conditions.

- *Business Processes.* The term business process refers to the overall work flow within a company and includes elements such as product design, manufacturing, and delivery. A good process analysis will help a leadership team to see what must be done given the company's strategy, and how those processes can be improved.

- *Capabilities.* Capabilities are bundles of separate skills required to deliver the products or services that give a business competitive advantage. There are two parts of a capability assessment. First, the capabilities needed to execute the strategy must be determined. Second, the current level of ability in terms of those capabilities must be assessed. Without knowing what capabilities should be focused on and improved, competitive advantage will be difficult to achieve.

- *Organization Design and Resourcing.* This part of the analysis looks at alignment issues between the environment, the strategy, the skills required to achieve that strategy, and the organization structure. During this step, a management team can design an organization that aligns systems in a way that will allow them to execute a strategy. Unless the systems within a business are aligned to improve effectiveness or efficiency, strategy statements are merely plaques on the wall that are seldom realized.

- *Culture.* Culture refers to the set of shared values that influence behavior and direction over time. The style of management and the beliefs and assumptions commonly held by people in the organization must be determined in order to ensure alignment and execution of the strategy.

The steps required for the organization assessment grow out of these elements. Those steps will be described in detail in the pages that follow.

STEPS IN COMPLETING AN ORGANIZATIONAL ASSESSMENT

The model shown in Figure 7 is a visual and detailed overview of the organizational assessment. Before describing each step in detail, it is important to note that the model in Figure 7 is neither linear nor all-inclusive. In most cases, members of the leadership team or other study teams examine each of parts of the model simultaneously. Some details in the model will be removed or added, depending on the audit objectives and needs of the organization. A strategy audit team should decide as a group how much information is needed and then gather the data accordingly. However, most of the information should be gathered before moving into the organization design and resourcing phase of the audit since that information is essential to design.

This stage of the strategy audit should include the following steps:

Step 1: Clarify the Strategy

Step 2: Measure Viability and Robustness

Step 3: Outline Business Processes

Step 4: Determine Capabilities

Step 5: Determine Appropriate Organization Design and Resourcing

Step 6: Assess the Company's Culture

Step 7: Integrate the Elements of the Organization Assessment

---

FIGURE 7
ORGANIZATIONAL ASSESSMENT

STEP 1: STRATEGY CLARIFICATION
1. Description of the Business
2. Strategic Objectives
3. Mission, Vision, Values
4. Customers/Not, Products/Not, and Markets/Not
5. Beliefs and Assumptions
6. Analogous Industries
7. Changes Rules of the Game
8. Distinctiveness

STEP 2: VIABILITY & ROBUSTNESS
1. Market Viability
2. Financial Viability
3. Sustainability
4. Measures
5. Future Mapping/Scenario Analysis

STEP 3: BUSINESS PROCESSES
1. Macro Work Flow
2. Process Analysis
3. Best Practices

STEP 4: CAPABILITIES
1. Capabilities Needed
2. Current Capabilities
3. Development Plan

STEP 5: ORGANIZATION DESIGN & RESOURCING
1. Alignment
2. Gathering Alignment Data
3. Structure
   - Org. Chart
   - Real Struct.
4. Organizing around Processes
5. Resourcing Decisions

STEP 6: CULTURE ASSESSMENT
1. Company History
2. Beliefs and Assumptions
3. Leadership Style
4. Ability to Change

STEP 7: INTEGRATION & IMPLEMENTATION
1. Implementation Plan
2. Resourcing Strategy
3. Structure Requirements
4. Create Buy-in
5. Stakeholder Communication
6. Start with Core Processes
7. Common Mistakes

CLARIFY THE STRATEGY

The purpose of strategy clarification is to determine four things: a description of the business, a description of the strategy, how the firm is distinct or how it gains advantage, and the clarity of the strategy throughout the organization.

Description of the Business

A description of the business includes information about what industry the company is in, what niche(s) the company competes in, what part of the industry management has decided to focus on, the strategic objectives of the business, and the mission, vision, and values of the firm. Management can usually describe or provide written documentation about each of the above areas. The study team should also ask some of the questions below about what the business does and what it does *not* do. By determining what the business does not do, the direction of the business and what it has decided to focus on becomes more clear.

• What products do we offer, and what products do we not offer?

• What customers do we pursue, and what customers are we not interested in?

• What markets do we focus on, and what markets do we avoid?

• What have we stopped doing in the last few years and why?

The study team should try to determine if the stated goals of the business depict what actually happens in day-to-day operations. If a discrepancy exists, it should be noted for future design. Discrepancies are usually a sign of misaligned support systems or miscommunication.

If the strategy is not clear, or if managers want to change the company's strategy, the leadership team may find it helpful to examine its own beliefs and assumptions, along with beliefs and assumptions that are held industry-wide about how competitive advantage is gained. If traditional ways of doing things are limiting a company's performance, then challenging either industry or organizational beliefs and assumptions by doing business differently can lead to competitive advantage. For example, when Canon entered the copier business, executives at Xerox believed that the only way to sell copiers was to have direct sales and service representatives that set up agreements to lease their copiers. Canon challenged this assumption and made an inexpensive, high-quality copier that needed little service and required little initial capital investment. The result? As Canon quickly gained market share, Xerox was forced to change the way it did business.

Strategy Description and Clarity

Besides describing what business an organization is in, the leadership team should also describe what strategy the company is pursuing in that business. Without strategy, managers have no framework by which to make decisions. Therefore, it becomes difficult to prioritize internal initiatives, determine the value of initiatives, decide where to commit resources, and decide when to say "no" to opportunities or developments. The easiest way to determine an organization's strategy is to find the strategic direction and strategic objective statements often published by upper management. If these statements exist and people are available to describe the direction and objectives in more detail (such as upper management or people from the planning group), the leadership team's job is easy. However, if no such documents exist, or if they are vague and nondescript, it will be necessary to interview people that have been in the organization for an extended period of time.

Team members may also want to review presentations that have been made to investors where strategy has been described, or look at decisions that have been made historically. It is also important to determine which products or markets the organization has withdrawn from, especially when getting out of a market has affected the company's direction. The rationale behind such decisions can provide insight into what the organization currently does and why.

Another aspect of strategy clarification is determining how clear the strategy is in the minds of people throughout the organization. Unless the strategy is clear to those who actually implement it, the process of developing a strategy will be nothing more than an academic exercise with little benefit to the business. However, care should be taken not to dismiss a strategy because a company appears to have little focus. It is quite possible that the lack of focus is due to problems in the company's communication process or in the organization's design and not because of the strategy itself. To determine where the problem is, the team should ask employees (those in charge of implementing the strategy) how they interpret and describe the company's strategy, what problems they see with the strategy, and how what they are asked to produce compares with what they are rewarded for. This may provide significant insights into what the company's actual strategy is, how well it is being communicated, and how people on the front lines think that it could be improved.

Distinctiveness and Advantage

One mark of a successful strategy is that it distinguishes a company from its competitors by creating advantage in the marketplace. If organizations do not make a specific effort to determine how to prioritize initiatives and commitment of resources, they become unfocused and their performance is mediocre. Likewise, organizations that spend all of their resources and time trying to do everything well end up being viewed by customers as following a "me too" strategy that offers nothing different, unique, or better in comparison to other players in the market. The consequence of either action is that customers have no compelling reasons to develop a loyal relationship with the company.

Businesses that have competitive advantage in the marketplace have usually made a conscious effort to achieve world-class performance in a certain area. Businesses that are unclear about their strategy are also unclear about how to focus resources and management effort in order to become world class.

Sources for Finding Strategy Clarification Information

There are a number of sources available to audit teams that will help them find much of the data needed to find the information outlined above. These sources are listed in Figure 8.

Figure 9 gives a list of suggested questions that can be asked of experts, in-house specialists or planning group members. They can also be used as questions to guide research in reports and periodicals.

The audit team should determine what kind of information is needed to best complete the strategy audit. The team might decide to use all of these sources or very few of them, depending on the objectives of the audit and the time and resources available. For example, the culture of one company caused people to feel uncomfortable with analysis and decision making processes that weren't based on large amounts of data,

FIGURE 8
SOURCES AVAILABLE TO AUDIT TEAMS

SOURCES	USES	TIME REQUIREMENT
ANNUAL REPORTS	Strategy description	Minimal
	Description of the business	
	Distinctiveness	
RECRUITING LITERATURE	Strategy description	Minimal
	Description of the business	
	Current performance	
SURVEYS		Moderate
- Upper management	Strategic clarity	
- Employees	Alignment	
INTERVIEWS	Strategy description	Significant
- Upper management	Business description	
- Suppliers	Customer data	
- Industry analysts	Distinctiveness	
- Employees	Alignment	

almost to the point of excess. However, the organization has also been overburdened with surveys that regularly ask people for input and comments. We felt that a strategy clarification survey might have been inappropriate for this organization, since it would have been viewed by employees as "just another survey to keep me from doing my work." In this case, the audit team focused more on interviews of people outside the organization and document analysis as ways to gather the data needed.

FIGURE 9
QUESTIONS TO ASK IN STRATEGY CLARIFICATION

1. What (if anything) gives this business distinctiveness?

2. What skills does this business currently have that are better than those of the competition? Can this advantage be sustained for a period of more than a few years?

3. How is this company generally regarded in the industry or by outside experts? How do outsiders see the company's strategy? What do they think about it?

4. What are this company's strengths in creating a world-class organization?

5. What are the biggest roadblocks to this business becoming a world class organization?

6. What does the company do? Why?
   What does it not do? Why not?
   Who are its customers/Who are not its customers?
   What are its products/What are not its products?
   What are its markets/What are not its markets?

7. Why is the company in this business and not another?

8. Why is the company focusing on these customers and not others? Why is it making these products (or providing these services) and not others?

9. What direction do the company's vision, mission, and strategic objectives statements suggest?

10. Does this business have more than one strategy?

MEASURE VIABILITY
AND ROBUSTNESS

As industries change, so must business objectives and strategies. Strategies should not be completely revised every year, but they should gradually evolve to keep pace with new requirements. Viability and robustness testing helps audit teams determine current performance and future industry requirements. Current viability refers to current market share, success ratios, and return on investment of the present strategy. Future viability and robustness refers to testing of business strategies against future industry or world scenarios. By having key measures about current performance and future requirements in place, managers can ensure implementation and proper feedback of vital data necessary to make adjustments to the strategy or its tactics.

Current Performance and Viability

Current performance and viability looks at the alignment between the environment, the strategy, and the organization. Current performance should be assessed against organizational objectives and goals. To determine current performance, ask the following questions:

• Is the organization meeting its strategic objectives?

• What areas in the business have exceeded expectations? Why?

• Which areas need improvement?

• How does the performance of the business compare to that of competitors?

• How does the company's current performance compare to its past performance?

Helpful sources of information in this analysis includes figures describing the company's market share, success rates, cycle time, or other ratios specific to the business. Sources where this information can be found include annual reports, industry reports, internal financial statements, marketing analysis, etc.

Future Performance and Viability

The current strategy's *future* performance (or a new strategy's future performance) should also be ascertained. The ability of a strategy to perform in the future under different scenarios makes a strategy viable and robust. To determine robustness, the leadership team should brainstorm different scenarios that describe possible changes in the future business environment. They should brainstorm contrasting scenarios such as price increases, price decreases, retail domination, wholesale domination, constrained resources, increased government regulation, increased international competition and the opening or collapse of world markets. The purpose of this exercise is to develop four or five unique scenarios that describe possible changes in the business environment.

The next step is to test the business's strategy for its market viability in each scenario generated. The audit team should ask questions such as "Will competitive density increase or decrease?", "Will our capture rate increase or decrease?", "Will this strategy make us distinct?", "Will it provide customers with what they want?"

Next, future financial viability should be determined by looking at the returns received on the money required to do business. To help determine future financial viability, the team should ask the following questions:

• Is the firm making more money than it is investing in daily operations? If not, why?

• In order to increase these returns, what must be done?

• What are the factors that influence the return on investments?

• Which factors need to be emphasized or improved?

• In which scenario will this strategy lead to more sales, lower costs, higher profits, lower entry costs, or decreased lead time? (Note: there may be other measures more specific to a given business that the audit team should examine and monitor in the future in order to ensure alignment with the direction of the business.)

Shell Oil successfully used this technique to prepare for changes in the oil industry. Shell developed scenarios that described changes in the industry that made maintaining a strong position in the industry seem impossible at the time. However, when oil prices dropped

---

FIGURE 10
QUESTIONS TO ASK IN STRATEGY CLARIFICATION

1. Does this strategy give us the market share we need and expect?

2. What kind of demand is there for this product or service?

3. Will this strategy provide sustainable competitive advantage?

4. Will this strategy help us accomplish our strategic objectives?

5. What kind of future opportunity is there if this strategy is followed?

6. What are the vulnerabilities of this strategy?

7. Is this strategy consistent with the environment and changing customer needs?

8. What value does this give our shareholders?

9. How does this strategy fare in future mapping or scenario analysis?

10. How easily and quickly can this strategy be copied?

unexpectedly, Shell was one of the few companies that were prepared because managers had played out their strategy under a similar scenario and knew how to respond.

Figure 10 outlines additional questions to be asked by the audit team in assessing viability and robustness.

OUTLINE
BUSINESS
PROCESSES

There are certain processes in every business that must exist in order to deliver products and services to the customer, either internal or external. Strategy helps business leaders decide which of those processes should be emphasized in order to distinguish the company in the marketplace.

Competitors in an industry pursue different priorities in order set themselves apart from others who provide similar products or services. The athletic shoe industry illustrates how companies distinguish themselves. Nike led the industry for a number of years by selling a variety of quality sport shoes. Reebok entered the industry and quickly eroded Nike's market share by focusing on a different part of the process — fashion and marketing. While Nike continued to emphasize design and R&D to produce its high quality athletic shoes, Reebok started designing comfortable, fashionable shoes that were at parity with Nike in quality. By focusing its efforts on processes different from those emphasized by Nike, Reebok was able to create shoes that quickly attracted aerobic enthusiasts.

Competition between the Nike and Reebok has caused both companies to improve their quality, design, styling, and marketing abilities. However, each company has remained focused on different processes in selling athletic shoes. This difference in focus has made both companies distinct.

Macro Work Flow

To decide which processes a business should focus on, the audit team should construct macro work flows for delivering products or services to the customer. A macro work flow includes everything from the initial conceptualization of a product idea all the way through to sales and service. Two different hypothetical examples are shown in Figure 11, one for the athletic shoe industry and the other for the real estate industry. These examples are not all-inclusive.

A good strategy will define how a business gains distinctiveness in the eyes of customers, what is different about the relationship a business will have with its customers versus the relationship competitors have with customers, and what must be emphasized to gain competitive advantage. After a team has determined the macro work flow, it should determine what part of that work flow should be emphasized given the strategy. A business cannot do everything in the macro work flow well. Attempting to excel at everything will constrain resources and dilute focus. Organizations that focus their efforts and resources typically become distinct and

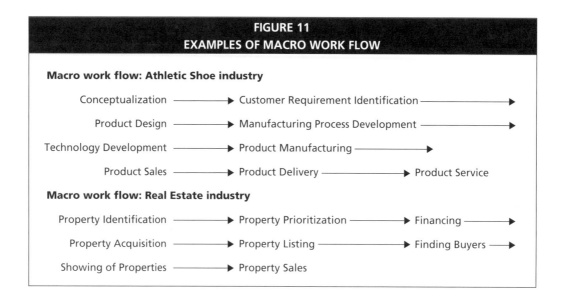

advantaged in their industry. For a business to become world-class, managers need to decide what part of the work flow they will focus on. For example, Nike does not manufacture the shoes it sells; it allows other companies that focus on world-class manufacturing to make its products.

Process Analysis and Improvement

The processes in the macro work flows can be divided into the following four categories:

- Unit of competitive advantage (UCA) work: distinguishes a company from its competitors and creates an advantage for it in the market. From the examples used earlier, this includes product design for Nike or marketing for Reebok.

- Value-added support work: facilitates the accomplishment of the UCA work. For example, the development of an effective information management system may not result in competitive advantage for a company, but it may support an area of focus that does create advantage, such as customer service.

- Essential support work: neither creates advantage nor facilitates the work that creates advantage, but must be done if businesses are to continue to operate. Examples of essential support work could include paying taxes or maintaining accounting records.

- Non-essential work: creates disadvantage for a business because it is work that has lost its usefulness but continues to be done because of tradition.

Process analysis gives audit teams a framework for improvement decisions. The team should first decide which processes are core to the business and which are support work. Managers should then concentrate on improving the core processes to a performance level that exceeds that of competitors. This type of improvement will ensure success in the marketplace. Managers should then be very clear about what is support work to the business and perform that work at parity with the competition.[1] The level of capability required in core work and support work will vary and should be looked at carefully. Capability analysis will be considered later in this guide.

Process Improvement through Best Practices Analysis

Best practices is similar to but slightly different from benchmarking: compare a company's practices with those of other businesses and learn how to improve performance. *Best practices* analysis is used to learn about analogous processes from similar organizations, or from organizations engaged in similar activities. An interchange is devised in a best practices analysis whereby businesses can exchange good ideas about what has and has not worked for them. Best practice analysis focuses more on *how things get done* than on *what gets done*; it focuses more on the overall secret of success than on particular process improvements; and it looks more at qualitative than quantitative issues.

Benchmarking, on the other hand, implies a continuing relationship whereby a business studies the specific functions of unmatched examples of excellence. For example, "What can our shipping department learn from that of L.L. Bean?" The process in the benchmarked organization becomes a role model or standard by which improvement in performance is measured. The analysis in benchmarking is more quantitative than the analysis in best practices.

Sharing best practices between organizations can often lead to process improvement and to new ways of thinking about the business — ideas that can lead to competitive advantage in the marketplace. However, the trap presented by sharing best practices is that leaders who visit another business may see an overwhelming number of good practices that they would like to duplicate. Many of those ideas might not be applicable to the strategy. For example, the comment of one senior manager after a visit to Motorola was, "We should start a Motorola University here!" In reality, such a university at his company would probably not lead to advantage in the eyes of the customer. Even though establishment of a company university was a very exciting concept, it would not improve the core work of the business. Before adopting best practices, managers should ask: Would it dilute or leverage resources? Is it core to our business? Does it leverage the UCA? and Can other companies provide the service to the client more effectively at a lower cost? Insights gained from best practice studies should not be incorporated unless they fit into a company's strategy.

DETERMINE CAPABILITIES

Once the team has clarified the business's strategy, the processes that should emphasized, and requirements for future viability, the next step is to determine the capabilities required and whether or not they are currently available. The question central to this part of the audit is this: What are the required capabilities, and does the business have the necessary skills and capabilities to successfully execute the chosen strategy? If the capabilities don't currently exist in the business, then they must either be developed or a new strategy must be chosen. It is generally easier to implement a new strategy if a business already has some of the necessary skills and capabilities — especially if it already has an advantage based on those capabilities. However, the absence of those skills and the difficulty of developing capabilities should not rule out the pursuit of a good strategy. Instead, the merit of a particular strategy should be determined on the basis of whether or not the skills can be acquired, the cost of acquiring those skills, and the strategy's potential to create competitive advantage.

Capabilities Needed and Current State

Capabilities are different than skills. A skill is a proficiency in a specific area of expertise, such as paleontology in the field of geology. Capabilities are the combination of several skills designed to carry out a particular process, such as negotiating, which requires combined knowledge about the business, its processes, the industry, human nature, and selling. Whether choosing a new strategy or implementing an existing strategy, it is essential that after core processes have been outlined, capabilities need to be improved to a level that exceeds the performance of competitors in those processes and gives a business distinctiveness. Support work, which is outside the core processes, should be improved only to parity with competition. Otherwise, resources get diverted and diluted away from the key processes and capabilities required to gain competitive advantage.

For example, Harley-Davidson's strategy is to provide a lifestyle for motorcycle riders. As a result, it has improved the quality of its motorcycles only to parity with its competition. Honda motorcycle, on the other hand, focuses its efforts on the design and quality of its bikes. Honda makes technologically more sophisticated engines and motorcycle designs than Harley because of its strategy. Both companies are very clear about what capabilities give them advantage. Effort and resources are committed to gaining and improving those capabilities that lead to advantage and ensure success.

The first step in determining what capabilities are required is to look at the processes that give customers the bundle of products and services they want most. This can be done by reviewing the process analysis completed earlier. Managers should decide

FIGURE 12	
HELPFUL SOURCES FOR DETERMINING CAPABILITIES	
INTERNAL	EXTERNAL
Employees	Suppliers
Managers (especially country managers)	Partners
Other divisions	Industry experts
Internal reports	Professional organizations
Planning departments	Recruiters

what must be done to deliver those products at lower cost, better quality, superior service, or improved speed. The answers to these questions will indicate what capabilities are required.

The next step is to determine the level of capability an organization has in these core processes. This can be done by talking to a variety of people that are involved with the business, such as employees, suppliers, and customers. Figure 12 shows internal and external sources that can be helpful in determining capabilities. Figure 13 gives a

FIGURE 13
QUESTIONS TO ASK IN CAPABILITY ANALYSIS

1. What is this business really good at?

2. What skills does this business currently have that are better than those of competitors?

3. What capabilities are needed with this strategy? (This should be answered by looking at the key processes that create competitive advantage).

4. Where do customers say we need to improve?

5. What is the gap between current capabilities and capabilities needed to give the company advantage?

6. How easy is it to acquire or build the needed capabilities?

7. How much time and money will be needed to develop these skills?

8. What is the organizational impact of this skills transition?

9. Why have projects been lost and to whom were they lost?

10. Where and how is the competition beating the company?

11. What specific skills are contained within the capability bundles?

12. How are these capability bundles arranged to gain competitive advantage?

13. What programs does the company need or have in place that are designed to improve capabilities?

list of possible questions to be asked. However, team members should be careful about how much weight is given to each response. Interviewers should gather enough data from different perspectives to test the validity of what various respondents say. This should be done for both positive and negative comments. The capability validation process has proven to be difficult for many companies because it is difficult to determine conclusively whether a skill or capability is really better or worse than that of competitors or better or worse than it should be.

The final step in capability analysis is to develop a plan that will improve or acquire the capabilities required. Human Resource personnel can help identify what programs are currently in place. If capabilities need to be acquired or improved, the team should develop an appropriate plan. Remember, not every process within the business needs to be improved — only those that lead to competitive advantage. Trying to improve everything only dilutes focus and does not lead to distinctiveness in the marketplace.

Figure 14 illustrates the need for assessing capability. Many companies continue to do what they do very well without determining whether or not those capabilities fit customer requirements. Others respond to customer requests, moving into new areas of business without having the necessary skills. Both strategies are disastrous. An example of not matching skills with customer requirements is the buggy whip manufacturing company that kept making buggy whips at full production even as cars were rolling

FIGURE 14
THE NEED FOR ASSESSING CAPABILITIES

	Does it Fit Customer Requirements?	
	YES	NO
Does it Fit Our Capabilities? YES	Ideal	Common Strategic Mistake
Does it Fit Our Capabilities? NO	Tough	Dumb

off the production lines. Even though the company excelled in making buggy whips, the capabilities proved useless when demand decreased before the organization had modified its strategy.

Phillip Morris is another example — one of not having the capabilities necessary to pull off a new strategy. Phillip Morris was known for its consumer marketing and did extremely well in the tobacco industry (cigarettes). The company acquired the soft drink maker 7-Up thinking it could leverage its skills from the tobacco industry to the soft drink industry. However, after the investment failed to produce the anticipated returns, 7-Up was eventually sold at a price below what Phillip Morris had paid for it. What Phillip Morris executives did not realize was that the two industries are very different, and that different skills are required to be successful in each.

Strategic errors result when goods and services are produced that do not fit customer requirements. Likewise, it is difficult to offer products and services in an area where an organization has no skills. Obviously, the ideal position is to have capabilities that are in demand by customers. Businesses should try to move themselves into the upper left quadrant of Figure 14.

DETERMINE APPROPRIATE ORGANIZATION DESIGN AND RESOURCE ALLOCATION

Evaluating organization design and resource allocation bridges the gap between data-gathering and strategy implementation. At this phase, an audit team starts synthesizing the data gathered and determining how an organization should implement the audit results. The most critical element of organization design is alignment, which is the matching of organization processes to the strategy. One of the authors of this guide has regularly observed that organizations are perfectly aligned to produce whatever results they achieve. In other words, an organization's performance is directly related to how it is aligned. Audit teams need to evaluate the organization's design in terms of its ability to align internal rewards, support systems, feedback loops, etc., with the strategy of the business.

Alignment

In their book *Real-Time Strategy*, Perry, Stott, and Smallwood state that "The goal of aligning strategy [and organizations] is to diminish the loss of organizational energy that normally occurs when organizational structures and systems are misaligned with strategy. Effective alignment releases more of a business's human energy to drive strategic improvising. Because entropy affects organizations in much the same way that it affects matter and energy, aligning strategy is a continuous challenge. Organizations are always falling out of alignment and need to be realigned."[2]

Some common misalignments are shown in Figure 15. Misalignment 1 shows that the strategy is aligned with the external

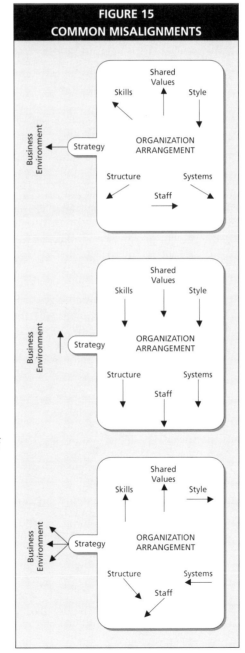

**FIGURE 15
COMMON MISALIGNMENTS**

FIGURE 16
DEFINITION OF MISALIGNMENT ELEMENTS

STRATEGIC INTENT: A concept that describes the organization's relationship with its customers. It distinguishes that relationship from the relationship competitors have with customers.

SHARED VALUES: A set of dominant and guiding values, beliefs and assumptions. The underlying basis for the organization's culture and character. It guides how the business thinks about stakeholders, suppliers, government agencies, community, employees and customers.

STRUCTURE: The formal organization chart (functional, customer, matrix, etc.) The relationships designating who reports to whom, layers of management, span of control, etc.

SYSTEMS: Routine processes and procedures such as information systems, rewards systems, measurement systems, planning systems, capacity scheduling systems, forecasting systems, budgets.

STAFF: Demographic description of important personnel categories within the organization such as age, career stage, gender, race, etc.

STYLE: Characteristic way that people behave in achieving the organization's goals. Describes how people at various levels spend time, and how they focus their attention.

environment, but everything else in the organization is moving in opposite directions. Misalignment 2 shows an organization perfectly aligned internally but not aligned with the environment (similar to the buggy whip example mentioned earlier). Misalignment 3 shows multiple strategies and chaotic internal systems. A definition of each of the elements within the models can be seen in Figure 16.

FIGURE 17
QUESTIONS TO ASK IN ASSESSING ORGANIZATIONAL DESIGN NEEDS

1. Describe your view of the current organizational strategy.

2. What parts of the organization are well-aligned to deliver the strategy?

3. Describe what current beliefs, policies, procedures, systems, or any other examples of misalignment that you may see.

4. What strategic initiatives are going well?

5. What are the things that get in the way of the organization implementing its strategy? (This may include structure, boundary issues, reward systems, capabilities, processes, information, etc.)

6. What are the things in the organization that are working well to support the implementation of the strategy?

7. What does the organization need to do better to execute the strategy effectively?

8. What gets in the way of people doing their work? Are there areas where effort is wasted?

9. How do people spend their time?

10. Where should efforts be focused to ensure competitive advantage?

11. What are the opportunity areas for improving efficiency and effectiveness?

FIGURE 18
SAMPLE STRATEGIC ALIGNMENT QUESTIONS

Respondents should rate the following statements on a scale ranging from "strongly disagree" to "strongly agree." These questions are copyrighted by Novations Group, Inc., and cannot be used without permission.

1. This organization does a good job of communicating its strategy to all employees.

2. This organization's management seems to balance long-term and short-term needs when making decisions.

3. Our technology (equipment, work flow, production processes) contributes positively to overall organization productivity.

4. The way work is organizationally assigned frequently leads to poor collaboration between work groups.

5. Much of my work is organized in such a way that I am able to function in an efficient manner.

6. I could do my job better if the information systems (reports, budgets, meetings, newsletters, etc.) in this organization kept me better informed.

7. People in my work unit spend too much time doing "busy work" instead of getting the real job done.

8. The bureaucracy in this organization seems to get in the way of me getting my work done.

9. Work units within this organization seem to be detrimentally competing against each other for resources (equipment, people, money, information).

10. If I do my job especially well, I will receive more financial rewards.

Gathering Alignment Data

The goal of the leadership team is to find misalignments and recommend organizational design changes that ensure continued alignment. There are three ways of determining how well the organization is aligned with its strategy and environment: focus groups, surveys, and interviews with managers and employees within the organization. Who else is better qualified to describe the misalignments within a business than those in charge of strategy implementation?

Extensive help in using each of these research methods is included in the Company Audit Guide, which accompanies this series. The goals of conducting focus groups, sending out surveys, and interviewing employees are to understand the employees' perception of the current strategy, identify areas of current organizational misalignment, and identify key issues or barriers related to the successful implementation of the strategy. Figure 17 lists questions that have been used in conducting focus groups and interviews. Figure 18 is a sample survey designed to gather alignment information.

Organizational Structure

When looking at alignment issues, it is also important to look at the organizational structure. This includes both the formal organization as reflected on the organization chart, and the actual or informal organizational structure. The personal relationships and political considerations that determine the informal structure often influence the way work is done as much as the formal structure planned by managers.

Managers often organize their companies around functional expertise which often leads to the development of functional silos. Another common factor in determining organization structure is the creation of positions or departments for senior people in search of a new role. Although these factors are part of the organizational reality, especially in times of downsizing and layoffs, audit teams should keep in mind that the most effective way to organize a business is around processes and types of work.

The audit team should revisit the macro work flow developed earlier to determine how the work actually occurs within those processes. The team should study the sequence in which work occurs, where the key problems in the process lie, where the interdependencies occur in the process (these are likely breakdowns), and which organizational units perform each piece of the work. The answers to these questions will help determine whether the current structure helps or hinders hand-offs, interdependencies, and the accomplishment of work. Most work cuts across organizational boundaries. If organizations are not willing to organize around critical work processes, then unnecessary hand-offs occur, inefficiencies and duplication sets in, and support work starts to dominate core work.

Resourcing Decisions

As discussed previously, some work processes are central to the company's strategy while other processes support the core work. One common question is whether a company needs to own all of its support processes, or whether some can be contracted out. The answer to this question depends on the type of support work, and on whether or not the work is proprietary to the company. Figure 19 is a matrix developed by Novations Group, Inc. It provides a decision tool about whether or not processes should be owned, or whether the work can be contracted to others.

FIGURE 19
RESOURCING MATRIX

	Value-Added Support	Essential Support
Proprietary	Provide	Maintain
Generic	Broker	Contract Out

Value-added support work facilitates the accomplishment of core work. Essential support work neither creates advantage nor facilitates core work, but must be done if businesses are to continue to operate. Both types of work may require capabilities that are proprietary to the business and capabilities that are generic, or that can be done by any firm. Decisions about where processes fall in the matrix should be made with the help of those people close to the work. In short, if the work is proprietary, it should remain in-house and be performed at the appropriate level of competency (world class, parity, or efficiency). If the work is generic, it can be contracted out, but should be monitored.

The benefit of contracting work out is two-fold. First, it allows managers to focus resources on improving the source of the company's competitive advantage. Second, it allows access to superior products and services offered by firms that make those offerings their core work.

ASSESS THE COMPANY'S CULTURE

Culture consists of the values, beliefs, and norms that manifest themselves in the habitual ways organization members accomplish their work, relate to one another, and solve the problems that confront them. Understanding a company's culture helps decision makers understand why choices have been made in the past, the ability and willingness of the organization to change, and the roadblocks to strategy implementation. As an audit team completes an organizational assessment, it should pay constant attention to the culture and ask why things are done the way they are and whether the culture is changing in any way.

Assessing a culture is a complex process. It involves skilled interviewing of a broad range of people throughout the organization. The goal of the assessment is to uncover the basic beliefs and assumptions that are widely shared in an organization, and to construct a picture of how the organization operates.

While an exhaustive culture audit is recommended as part of the strategy audit, audit team members may be able to piece together information reflecting fundamental aspects of the culture from a macro study. Care should be taken to avoid drawing conclusions that are not based on validated data, however. This chapter will mention a few elements of the culture that affect strategy implementation. They include the company's history, style, and beliefs, and assumptions. For a detailed methodology about auditing cultures, refer to *The Corporate Culture Audit* in this series.

Three Elements of a Culture Assessment

The leadership style, company history, and organizational beliefs and assumptions should be analyzed and understood before attempting to change a company's strategy. If changes in the strategy or organization are required, these three elements of culture can contribute to or detract from the strategy implementation. For example, if a business has historically resisted change, then implementing a radically different strategy will be very difficult. If the management style is autocratic, employees throughout the company may feel little ownership for new initiatives required to achieve the strategy, and may be reluctant to suggest ways of aligning the company. If challenging the beliefs and assumptions of top management is widely discouraged, companies are unlikely to come up with revolutionary ways of doing business. Consequently, audit teams should pay special attention to each of these elements of culture to ensure alignment, change in the organization, and successful implementation of strategic objectives.

INTEGRATE THE ELEMENTS OF THE ORGANIZATION ASSESSMENT

The following framework provides a systematic way of summarizing the findings of the organization assessment. This structure should be used to determine what organizational factors should be considered in strategy implementation.

FIGURE 20 INDUSTRY ANALYSIS		
ORGANIZATIONAL COMPONENT	FINDINGS	IMPACT
What is our strategy? How has it changed in the past five years? How is it likely to change in the future?		
How viable and robust is our business? How does our current strategy hold up under various future scenarios? What measures determine viability and robustness?		
What are our major business processes? What aspects of those processes should be emphasized given our strategy?		
What capabilities do we have now? Given our current strategy, what capabilities do we need to develop? What will it take to develop or acquire those capabilities?		
How well is our structure aligned with our strategy? Do our systems support our strategy? Are there systems that could be contracted out to others?		
Do our values and beliefs support the implementation of our strategy? How difficult will it be to accomplish the goals dictated by our strategy, given the way things are done in our company?		

Part 3

INTEGRATION AND IMPLEMENTATION

Both the environmental and organizational assessment portions of a strategy audit are designed to help corporate leaders understand the business they are in, what it takes to be successful in that business, and how to design an organization that can deliver products and services asked for by customers. By gathering information about stakeholders, customers, and competitors, a business is able to understand the overall environment in which it operates. By looking internally at current business operations, strategic objectives, and support systems, managers can understand where to focus resources and how to align the business to ensure distinctiveness in the eyes of customers. In short, these two data-gathering exercises provide the tools for anticipating fundamental shifts in the business environment, and what changes those shifts require from the organization.

By the time the two major parts of the audit have been completed, the task of integrating the findings is all that remains. In this process, audit team members should attempt to answer one fundamental question: Is our strategy in alignment with the external environment? In order to answer this broad question, the following issues should be discussed:

• Do our capabilities match our customer requirements?

• Do we offer something required by our customers that is better than the offerings of our competitors?

• How are customer demands changing?

• How are competitors changing?

• How are our internal capabilities evolving to keep pace with those changes?

As a strategy audit team completes the data gathering phase outlined in the environmental and organizational assessment sections, it needs to ask questions about the data's significance and validity. It should also consider the changes suggested by the data. Then, depending on the answers to these questions, the team can implement the changes dictated by the audit. Although the subject of implementation is complex, this guide concludes by offering four elements that managers should consider when making changes to the organization.

• *Structure follows strategy.*

Strategy defines an organization's objectives, and structure is the means of realizing those objectives. This concept implies that current organizational boundaries should not determine the selection of a competitive strategy. Instead, environment and organizational assessments should drive strategy selection. The organization is then designed to implement that strategy.

• *Plans for change must be widely owned.*

Those ultimately responsible for implementing strategy (typically front-line employees) should be consulted for their ideas about what changes should be implemented and how the implementation should take place. Otherwise, the best organization design will have little influence on strategy implementation if those required to make changes don't understand or agree with the changes.

• *Implementation should start with what is core to gaining advantage.*

Managers' first priority should be to improve core processes within the business. Performance in those processes should become world class. Support systems, while important, should only be emphasized if they lead to competitive advantage. Otherwise, support systems that remain in-house should be done at parity with competitors in order to avoid competitive disadvantage.

• *Avoid the following common mistakes:*

Expect all data to have the same usefulness.

Do nothing with the audit findings.

Do not link other support systems (rewards, administration, etc.) to strategy.

Do not think strategically about what processes and capabilities to keep in-house and what to outsource.

Give no priority to processes that must be world-class in order to gain advantage. Don't consider what must be done more efficiently to stay in business.

Fail to match internal capabilities with customer requirements and needs.

Fail to communicate the findings and strategy to people throughout the company in a simple, understandable manner.

Provide no useful framework for next steps.

References

1   For a more thorough discussion of this concept, see the article "Strategic Restructuring" by Gene Dalton, Lee Perry, Norman Smallwood and Jon Younger, published by Novations Group, Inc., Provo, Utah, USA, 1993.

2   Lee Perry, Randall G. Stott, and W. Norman Smallwood, Real-Time Strategy, John Wiley and Sons, 1993.

Part 4

THE AUDIT PROCESS

This section addresses the logistical and process requirements of conducting an audit. The topics covered in this section include:

- Staffing the audit team

- Creating an audit project plan

- Laying the groundwork for the audit

- Analyzing audit results

- Sharing audit results

- Writing effective audit reports

- Dealing with resistance to audit recommendations

- Building an ongoing audit program

STAFFING THE AUDIT TEAM

Who conducts the audit is as important in many ways as how the audit is conducted. In fact, the people selected for the audit team will, in large part, determine how the audit is done, how results are analyzed, and how findings are reported. The following list includes general characteristics of effective audit teams for most areas:

- Consists of three to four people.

- Reports to CEO or other senior executive.

- Represents a carefully selected range of skills and experience.

More than four people may be needed for an audit team if data gathering is labor intensive, as when large numbers of customers or employees must be interviewed. However, audit teams of more than six or seven people present problems of maintaining uniformity and communicating audit progress and findings during the course of the evaluation.

Selecting an Audit Team Leader

The audit team leader will play a strong role in shaping both the data gathering and the findings from the audit. The strength of the team leader will also influence the acceptance of the audit, both in terms of enlisting cooperation in the data gathering phase and in securing support for improvement initiatives that grow out of the audit. Because of the importance of this role, care should be taken in selecting the appropriate person for the job. The following qualities are found in successful audit team leaders:

- Has a good relationship with the CEO or with the executive-level sponsor of the audit.

- Is well-liked and well-respected at all levels of the organization, especially in the area to be audited.

- Has good interpersonal skills; can maintain good relationships even in difficult circumstances.

- Has good analytical skills; can assimilate and process large amounts of complex data quickly.

- Has some knowledge of the function or area being audited.

- Has extensive knowledge of the type of process being audited.

- Communicates ideas clearly and effectively.

Skills to Be Represented on the Audit Team

Once the team leader has been chosen, audit team members should be selected on the basis of what each can bring to the project. Selection efforts should focus on developing a balanced representation of the following qualities:

- A variety of tenures in the organization, with relative newcomers preferably having experience in other organizations.

- A variety of familiarity with the area (function or site) being audited. Those who are intimately familiar with the area can serve as guides to the less familiar; those who are new to the area can provide objectivity and ask questions that might never be considered by those more involved in the area.

- Considerable familiarity with the type of process being audited. For this reason, many organizations call on people filling roles in similar processes from other parts of the company to work on audit teams.

- Good analytical skills.

- Good interpersonal skills.

- Good facilitation and interviewing skills.

- Good communication skills.

- An understanding of the company's strategy and direction.

CREATING AN AUDIT PROJECT PLAN

Creating an audit project plan accomplishes the following objectives:

- Ensures the allocation of adequate resources, or helps audit team members be prepared to improvise in the face of short resources.

- Ensures the audit is timed so resources are available that may be in high demand.

- Creates clear expectations in the minds of team members about what must be done, and when — especially important when they are not committed to the project full-time.

- Ensures accountability for what must be done, who is responsible for which tasks, and when the audit must be completed.

Financial audits often rely on the Critical Path Method (CPM) of project planning. This method was originally developed by the US Department of Defense during World War II to facilitate the timely completion of weapons development and production. It has since been modified to plan a wide variety of projects. The following outline is a simplification of CPM. It suggests the aspects of a project that should be taken into account during the planning phase.

Critical Path Method

In developing the project plan, audit team members should ask and answer the following questions:

- *What tasks must be performed?*

This list should include the major tasks outlined in the audits, along with subtasks that grow out of those major headings. It should also include any tasks mandated by unique circumstances in the company performing the self-assessment. The audit team may want to brainstorm about tasks that need to be performed, then refine the list to reflect the work priorities of the audit.

• *In what order will the tasks be completed?*

Answering this question should include an analysis of which tasks and sub tasks are dependent on others. Which tasks cannot begin until another has been completed? Which tasks can be done at any time? The audit team may want to place the ordered task on a time line, with start dates, expected duration of the step, and end dates outlined for each task.

• *Who will perform each task?*

Most tasks will be performed by members of the audit team. These assignments should be made by taking the strengths of each team member into consideration, as well as the time availability of each person. Equity of work load should also be taken into account. If tasks are to be assigned to people not on the audit team, those individuals should be included or consulted at this point.

• *What resources will be needed for each step?*

Each task should be analyzed in terms of the personnel, budget, equipment, facilities, support services, and any other resources that will be needed for its completion. The team should assess the availability of all of the resources. Consideration should be given to the task ordering completed earlier. Are some resources subject to competing demands, and therefore difficult to secure at a particular time? How far in advance do arrangements for resources need to be made? Does the task order or time line need to be revised in light of what is known about resource availability?

• *Where is the slack time?*

Slack time is unscheduled time between dependent tasks. Slack provides a degree of flexibility in altering the start dates of subsequent tasks. Slack time signals that a task has a range of possible start dates. It is used to determine the critical path.

• *What is the critical path?*

The critical path in a project is the set of tasks that must be completed in a sequential, chronological order. If any task on the critical path is not completed, all subsequent tasks will be delayed. Delays at any point in the critical path will result in an equivalent delay in the completion of the total project.

Regardless of the method used to develop the project plan, no project, regardless how simple, is ever completed in exact accordance with its plan. However, having a project plan allows the team to gauge its progress, anticipate problems and determine where alternative approaches are needed.

LAYING THE GROUNDWORK FOR THE AUDIT

Once the team has been selected and a project plan developed, the audit leader should prepare those who will be involved in and affected by the audit for the team's visit or for data-gathering. The following steps will help the audit to run more smoothly:

Communicate Executive Support for the Audit

Demonstrating executive support for the audit accomplishes two goals. First, it increases the chances that those involved in the area being audited will cooperate with data gathering efforts. Second, it shows executive support for the area being audited and suggests a commitment to improving the area's performance.

In many companies, the audit is introduced by the executive sponsor of the audit by means of a memo. The memo should explain the purpose of the audit and ask for the support of everyone in the area being audited. This memo is distributed to everyone within the company who will be affected by or involved in the data gathering process. The most effective memos explain how the audit results will be used, reassuring those who will be responding to audit team requests about the motives of the audit. The credibility of such memos is also bolstered when previous audits have been acted upon with positive results.

Make Arrangements with the Area to Be Audited

The audit team leader should check with the appropriate manager in charge of the process or site being audited to arrange for any required on-site visits, interviewing, surveys, focus groups, or written information needed for the audit. The team leader should also explain the purpose, scope, and expected duration of the audit; review the project plan with the manager; and answer any questions the manager has about the audit.

The team leader should also work with the appropriate manager or managers to determine how the audit can be conducted with the least impact on the flow of work. This may include discussions about the timing of the audit, the options for data gathering, the availability of needed data, and possibilities for generating the necessary information quickly and easily. Finding ways to make data collection more efficient and effective is especially important when the audit is part of an ongoing program, rather than an isolated assessment.

Develop a Protocol or Checklist

A protocol or checklist can be used by the audit team to outline the issues that are central to the audit. Written guides can help the leaders of those areas being audited to prepare for the audit. A protocol represents a plan of what the audit team will do to accomplish the objectives of the audit. It is an important tool of the audit, since it not only serves as the audit team's guide to collecting data, but also as a record of the audit procedures completed by the team. In some cases, audit teams may even want to format the checklist in a way that allows them to record their field notes directly on the checklist.

The checklist should include no more than twenty major items, and checklists should be updated with each audit in order to ensure that the appropriate measures are taken. Items where improvement initiatives have been successful should be eliminated from the checklist, with newly identified possibilities for improvement opportunities added.

ANALYZING
AUDIT RESULTS

Discovering gaps between a company's targets and its actual performance is a relatively easy task. Tools are provided to assist audit teams in assessing their performance in a given area. In most cases, more opportunities for improvement will be uncovered by an audit than can be addressed by the resources and energy available. Therefore, one of the most difficult aspects of analyzing the results of an audit lies in determining which opportunities are the most important for managers to pursue.

Because resources and energy for pursuing improvement initiatives are limited, choices must be made about which options are most important. Sometimes these decisions are based on political winds in the company, or on what has worked well in the past, or on personal preferences of top management. However, scarce resources will be used more effectively if allocated to the areas where they will have the greatest impact. Managers must also determine the most effective way to approach initiatives. This section discusses criteria for prioritizing opportunities that grow out of audit findings.

The Novations Strategic Alignment Model

The mid-1980s saw the birth of the "excellence" movement, where many companies tried to achieve excellence in every area of endeavor. Although the movement created an awareness of the need for management improvements, it failed to consider that not all management processes are equal in terms of producing benefits. As a result, leading organizations in today's environment focus on performing well in a few core areas. Knowing what those core areas are depends on a clear vision of the company's strategy.

Strategic thinking about which areas should be improved involves much more than taking an inventory of current capabilities and weaknesses. If it did not, existing capabilities would always determine strategic objectives, and organizational growth and development would come to a halt. To set priorities strategically, companies must decide which improvement opportunities fall in the following categories:

• What to do themselves.

• What to do with someone else.

• What to contract others to do.

• What not to do.

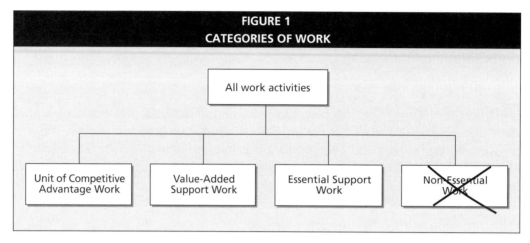

FIGURE 1
CATEGORIES OF WORK

Figure 1 illustrates the four categories of work.

Unit of Competitive Advantage (UCA) Work includes work and capabilities that create distinctiveness for the business in the marketplace.

Value-added Support Work facilitates the accomplishment of the UCA work. For example, a company may have a technology orientation rather than a service orientation, but an effective logistics process may help them to improve their UCA work of providing cutting edge technology.

Essential Support Work neither creates advantage nor facilitates the work that creates advantage, but must be done if businesses are to continue to operate (includes such things as paying taxes, maintaining payroll records, etc.).

Nonessential Work is activity that has lost its usefulness but continues to be done because of tradition.

Despite their sophistication in dealing with other aspects of business, most managers have archaic views of the different types of work. Many of their models for characterizing work have come from a finance or accounting orientation. Accounting terms such as overhead, direct labor, and indirect labor may be useful as a way to report costs, but they provide little understanding about the relative strategic importance of the work. Yet these classifications are frequently used to determine how work is organized and where resources are allocated.

The concept of *unit of competitive advantage* (UCA) helps to explain why some organizations either emphasize the wrong capabilities or de-emphasize the right capabilities. UCA also explains why some forms of improvement lead to competitive disadvantage, and why some businesses consistently outperform their competitors by gaining greater leverage from their competitive advantages.

A company's UCA includes the critical processes that create distinctiveness within an established strategic direction. It is based on the premise that businesses create competitive advantage when they focus their attention on a few key processes and implement those key processes in world-class fashion. For example, continuous improvement is a popular management program that assumes benefit from any kind of ongoing improvement. Generally speaking, however, continuous improvement programs will only create competitive advantage when an organization defines a strategic direction, clarifies strategic objectives, and determines its UCA. These crucial prerequisites tell where continuous improvement efforts should be focused to create maximum leverage. They suggest what kinds of work to improve interdependently, what kinds to improve separately, and what kinds not to waste time on. They even signal when continuous improvement is more likely to create competitive disadvantage rather than competitive advantage.

UCA Initiatives Should Take Priority

Understanding what work falls under which categories requires a clear understanding of the company's strategy. The initiatives resulting from an audit that affect the Unit of Competitive Advantage work processes should clearly have the highest priority among improvement projects. Value-added support initiatives should be second priority, and essential support work should be the third priority. Nonessential work should not be continued.

Once improvement opportunities that will have the greatest impact on the achievement of the company's goals have been identified, the following ideas can be used to lend further insight into how opportunities identified through an audit should be prioritized:

• *Focus on the two or three most important areas.*

Insisting that action be taken on all of the problems uncovered by the audit may overwhelm the people who are responsible for bringing about those changes. Flatter organizations and leaner work forces mean that people are already being asked to do more work with fewer resources and less time. Producing a long list of improvement initiatives may prompt people to dismiss all of them because they don't have time to complete the whole list.

• *Focus on the areas that can be changed.*

Emphasizing problems that are beyond the control of the people who are responsible to work on process improvement only leads to cynicism and a sense of powerlessness. By focusing on things that are within the sphere of influence, accountability for each part of the action plan can be clearly defined.

• *Include as priorities some improvements that can be made quickly.*

Rapid, visible improvement helps build support for more complicated initiatives. Quick improvements also reassure people of management's support for long-term improvement. Seeing immediate improvement helps to build commitment at all levels to the process, and helps build momentum for further change.

• *Emphasize the improvements that seem essential to long-term success.*

Essential improvements may involve sensitive issues or difficult problems, such as deficiencies in fundamental skill levels within the organization or basic strategy issues. These problems are not only difficult and expensive to address, but may also cause a great deal of personal pain or require significant individual adjustment. Nevertheless, long-term improvement requires a commitment to dealing with difficult issues rather than avoiding them.

SHARING AUDIT RESULTS

In most cases, audit results will be presented to various interested people in a feedback meeting. Those in attendance may include members of the executive team, managers who work in the area covered by the audit, the audit team members, and anyone else who is affected by or interested in the results. The meeting should be conducted by members of the audit team. The purpose is to present their findings, and make recommendations for capitalizing on opportunities for improvement.

Conducting Effective Feedback Meetings

The audit team's strategy for the meeting should be to present a clear and simple picture of the current situation as revealed by the audit. This may be a moment of truth for those who have been anticipating the audit results. The feedback meeting for an audit holds both excitement and anxiety: excitement that the future will be bright, and anxiety that shortcomings in individual performance will be highlighted and demands made for personal change. As a result, the meeting must be carefully managed in order to lead to productive change. The following structure is one recommended format for conducting a feedback meeting.

• *Introduce the meeting and preview its agenda.*

This might include an overview of the original intent of the audit, introduction of the audit team, and a brief summary of the meeting's agenda. This step should take no more than five minutes.

• *Present the audit findings.*

Audit findings should summarize the most important points revealed by the data gathered in the audit process. They should be presented separately from the audit recommendations in order to allow people to digest the two parts of the presentation separately. Clearing up misunderstandings about the findings may make the group more accepting of the team's recommendations.

The presentation of the audit findings should take comparatively little time. Audits almost always generate much more data than can be effectively presented or digested in a feedback meeting. The goal of the audit team should be to zero in on the two or three most important points learned from the audit, and present enough supporting data to illustrate those points.

Presenting too much data about audit findings has a number of negative effects. It encourages people to conduct their own analysis of the audit data. To a certain extent, this is a healthy and normal reaction. If others understand the evidence that supports the conclusions drawn by the audit team, they are more likely to accept and own the audit results. Therefore, they will be more committed to the changes brought about by the audit results. However, when people immerse themselves in large amounts of data, they may become victims of "analysis paralysis": they may spend unnecessary time attempting to explain contradictory data, or trying to understand methods used by others to gather data.

• *Present audit recommendations.*

Presenting the audit recommendations should be the central point of the meeting. The recommendations should grow out of the data highlights presented. The audit team should view the recommendations as discussion points for the meeting, rather than as absolute action items.

A common mistake in feedback meetings is to spend most of the meeting on presenting data and recommendations. It is easy for audit team members to become enamored of data they have invested considerable time and energy to collect and analyze. Others in the audience will probably also be interested in the details of the data collected. However, if too much time is spent on discussing the recommendations, the meeting will end before a commitment to action has been made.

• *Ask others to react to the data.*

The reactions of top management and those responsible for implementing audit recommendations will determine the ultimate value of the audit data. Therefore, the feedback meeting is a good time to resolve questions or problems with the findings and recommendations as they have been presented. If resistance to the audit findings is not resolved in the feedback meeting, opportunities for improvement may be lost.

Those attending the meeting may offer their opinions willingly. If not, the audit team members should ask the others in the room for their reaction to what has been presented.

• *Develop preliminary action plans.*

The detailed action plans should grow out of the recommendations made by the audit team. They should specifically address the question of who should do what by when. Formal accountability mechanisms should be established before the end of the meeting, such as the scheduling of subsequent meetings or follow-up check points.

70

WRITING EFFECTIVE AUDIT REPORTS

There are three fundamental purposes for writing a formal report at the conclusion of an audit:

- An audit report may be a stand-alone summary of the audit. This approach is not recommended, inasmuch as the report is likely to be filed away, making the probability of action unlikely.

- The report may supplement a feedback meeting, providing those in attendance with documentation and an outline to follow.

- The report should also serve as a baseline document to make measurement of performance improvement possible in future audits.

Because the written report is the most enduring part of the audit presentation, it should be well written and easy to understand. The following tips will lead to the preparation of effective written audit reports.

Focus on a Few Key Points

The audit presentation should focus on the two or three most important findings. It is impossible to present all of the data gathered in the audit to those who were not on the audit team. It is also not advisable to present every detail of the data. The audit team members should trust their own judgment about what the highlights of the study were, and present enough data to support that judgment. For each of the major findings, the team may want to include the following information:

- What is the problem?

- Why does it exist?

- What happens if the problem is not fixed:
  — in the short term?
  — in the long term?

- Recommend solutions.

- Outline expected benefits.

Prepare an Outline Before Writing the First Draft

A good outline ensures that the logic of the report is clear, and that ideas proceed in an order that makes sense. The following outline provides one approach that works effectively.

Background

This section should establish the framework for the audit in terms of:

• Providing a brief discussion of the overall purpose of the audit.

• Identifying the role of the audit team in the overall process.

• Establishing the limitations of the audit methodology to ensure that others utilize the results provided in the report appropriately.

Objectives

This section should identify specific objectives of the audit in terms of types of information the team was expected to generate.

Methodology

The methodology section should describe the mechanics of the audit and include the following information:

• Types of assessment used (survey, interviews, focus groups, etc.).

• Data sources, or the sample groups for each of the types of assessment used.

• Time frame during which the audit was conducted.

• Other pertinent details about how the audit was conducted.

Findings

This section is designed to provide others with a review of the "facts" that came out of the audit. Except in cases where an audit checks regulatory compliance, only the most significant findings should be discussed in any detail in the report. This section should also include briefly presented data supporting the findings.

Conclusions

This section should report the audit team's interpretation of what the facts of the audit mean in light of the objectives stated at the outset of the audit.

Recommendations

This section includes suggestions from the audit team on how to close the performance gaps identified in the audit. The degree of specificity to be included in the audit report will vary from company to company and audit to audit.

Appendix

This portion of the formal report should include any of the following items that are relevant to the audit:

• A copy of any questionnaires or survey instruments used in the audit.

• A summary of the data gathered in the course of the audit.

• Recommendations for subsequent audits based on the team's experience.

Present Audit Findings Accurately

Those who read the report will no doubt be somewhat familiar with the area covered by the audit. They may notice discrepancies between what they know about the subject and what is reported in the written document. Spotting one inaccuracy may lead the readers to discredit all of the findings, conclusions and recommendations. Audit team members should be careful to report data as it was actually generated, and to describe the impact of the findings accurately.

Use Clear, Concise Language

Every statement included in the report should be based on sound evidence developed or reviewed during the audit. Whatever is said must be supported or supportable. Speculation should be avoided. Generalities and vague reporting will only confuse and mislead those that the report should influence or inform. For example, a report using the terms *some*, *a few*, or *not all* can leave the reader confused about the significance of the finding. Specific quantities should be used, such as, "of the ten samples taken, two were found to be...", "Three of five respondents said that...", and so on. Statements should be qualified as needed, and any unconfirmed data or information should be identified as such.

Ideas or sentences that do not amplify the central theme should be eliminated. The report should not identify individuals or highlight the mistakes of individuals.

Use Good Grammar and Style

Basic grammar and style rules should be followed in writing the text. Below are some examples:

- Avoid extreme terms, such as alarming, deplorable, gross negligence, etc.

- Avoid using redundant or lengthy phrases, such as calling something an emergency situation when the word emergency alone will do.

- Avoid verbs camouflaged as nouns or adjectives. For example, use "the new procedure will reduce error entries," rather than "The new procedure will accomplish a reduction of error entries."

- Avoid indirect expressions where possible. For example, "Many instances of poor management were found," is more direct than saying, "There were many instances of poor judgment found."

- Use short, familiar words. Use words that are easily understandable to everyone and that convey the message concisely.

- Keep sentences short. Most writing experts suggest that an average sentence should be between 15 and 18 words. Packing too many ideas into a single sentence confuses and tires readers.

The audit team should provide enough background information in the report so that the reader clearly understands who conducted the audit and what the audit did or did not include. The purpose of the report as well as the purpose and scope of the audit should also be described in a manner that enables the reader to know why the report was written and who should take corrective action.

Timing of the Report

The timing of audit reports is critical to the overall reporting process and must be carefully thought out. In many cases, a written draft of the audit report is prepared one to three weeks before the feedback meeting. This draft then goes through a review and another report is prepared in time for the team's presentation. A final report may be completed after the feedback session has been held in order to record changes resulting from that meeting.

DEALING WITH RESISTANCE TO RECOMMENDATIONS

Most audit teams feel that if they can present their ideas clearly and logically, and have the best interests of the company or department at heart, managers will accept the recommendations made as part of the audit and follow the team's recommendations. Many people who have worked in organizations, however, find that no matter how reasonably recommendations are presented, they are all too often not implemented.

Implementation usually fails because it requires people to change their ways of working. That change requires a great deal of effort, energy, and risk; therefore, change is usually resisted. Resistance is an emotional process; people may embrace recommendations based on their logic, but fail to implement them because of the emotional resistance to the personal change involved. Resistance is a predictable, natural, and necessary part of the learning process. Although resistance may cause audit team members to feel they have missed the mark in terms of the recommendations they have made, it actually often signals accuracy in having interpreted the organization's needs. By dealing with the resistance directly, audit teams can work through barriers to implementing process improvements.

What Are the Signs of Resistance?

In many cases, resistance may be expressed directly. Direct objections to recommendations are relatively easy to address, inasmuch as they can be discussed and resolved. When recommendations are being presented, team members should stop frequently to allow those who are listening to the report to voice any objections or disagreements. Those who are presenting the data should be careful not to become defensive or to punish those who express reservations about the recommendations. It is impossible to deal with objections unless they are voiced; therefore, the audit team should welcome the expression of objections or differences of opinion. The following tips may be used for surfacing and dealing with direct resistance:

• Provide many opportunities for others to express their concerns.

• Carefully clarify any confusing concerns.

• Deal with important or easy concerns immediately. Defer the remainder.

• Summarize the concerns before moving on. Show that concerns have been heard.

- It may even be helpful to list concerns on a flip chart or blackboard.

If direct resistance continues, the following steps may be necessary:

- Talk about the differences of opinion.

- Voice concern and support for negotiating a resolution.

- Avoid struggles for control of the situation.

Dealing with Indirect Resistance

In other cases, resistance may be subtle and elusive. Indirect resistance is difficult to identify and deal with because its manifestations seem logical. People who are experiencing indirect resistance may feel that they are "getting the run around." Many different forms of resistance may manifest themselves in a single meeting:

- Request for more detail.

- Providing too much detail in response to questions.

- Complaining that there isn't enough time to implement recommendations.

- Claiming that the recommendations are impractical.

- Attacking those who propose improvement initiatives.

- Acting confused.

- Responding with silence.

- Intellectualizing about the data.

- Moralizing that problems wouldn't exist if it weren't for "those people".

- Agreeing to implement recommendations with no intention of acting on them.

- Asking questions about methodology.

- Arguing that previous problems have resolved themselves.

- Focusing on solutions before findings are fully understood.

Almost any of these responses is legitimate in moderate amounts. For example, members of the group may have concerns about the audit's methodology that should be considered. Managers may realistically wonder where they will find the time to implement recommendations. However, if refusal to act on recommendations persists once legitimate concerns have been addressed, then the audit team is probably facing indirect resistance.

Many models used in sales training provide recommendations for overcoming resistance. These methods suggest the use of data and logical arguments to win the point and convince the other person to buy whatever is being sold. These models work well for direct resistance. However, indirect resistance is normally based on feelings rather than logic. Therefore, the only way to truly overcome resistance is to deal with the emotional processes that cause it to happen in the first place. It is almost impossible to talk people out of the way they feel.

Feelings pass and change when they are expressed directly. A key skill for audit teams that are attempting to implement recommendations is to ask the people who are presenting resistance to put directly into words what they are experiencing. The most effective way to make this happen is for the audit team members to address directly what is happening in the situation. The following keys provide help in surfacing and dealing with indirect resistance.

- *Work once or twice with the person's concern, even when it feels as if he or she is resisting recommendations.*

By attempting to work with the problem stated by the person raising a concern, audit team members can determine whether the concern is legitimate or whether it is an excuse for not taking action. If the issues raised are legitimate, the person should show some willingness to discuss and resolve them. If the issues are manifestations of indirect resistance, the person will probably respond with other forms of resistance.

- *Identify the form the resistance is taking.*

Paying attention to the dynamics of a discussion can provide important clues as to whether or not a person is resisting recommendations. If a person is consistently distancing him or herself from those who are presenting the audit findings, using gestures or postures that suggest tension or discomfort, while at the same time presenting arguments for why the recommendations presented are inappropriate, it is probably a sign of resistance. The non-verbal responses of the presenters may also signal the onset of resistance. If presenters feel that they are suppressing negative feelings or becoming bored or irritated, it may be further evidence that the client is resisting.

Once presenters become aware of the resistance, the next step is to put it into words. This is best done by using neutral, everyday language. The skill is to describe the form of the resistance in a way that encourages the person to make a more direct statement of the reservation he or she is experiencing.

One general rule for stating what type of resistance is being manifested is to phrase the statement in common, non-threatening language. Statements should be made in the same tone and language that would be used to address a problem with a spouse or close friend. The statement should be made with as little evaluation as possible; it is the presenter's observation about what is happening in the situation.

A second general rule for surfacing indirect resistance involves not talking for a couple of moments after the presenter has stated what he or she has observed. There may be a temptation to elaborate on the observation, or to support it with evidence. However, continuing the statement will reduce the tension in the situation. Without tension, the person who is resisting feels no discomfort, and is unlikely to address the issue directly. Moreover, elaborating on the original statement may increase the other person's defensiveness and reduce the chances of solving the problem.

If stating the problem in direct, non-punishing terms fails to bring the resistance out into the open, there may be little more the audit team can do to overcome the indirect resistance. The best strategy in this case is to avoid resisting the resistance. Team members should support the person who is resisting and proceed with the implementation of recommendations to the extent possible.

BUILDING AN ONGOING AUDIT PROGRAM

As the pace of change increases, and as organization leaders become more and more committed to continuously improving their effectiveness and efficiency, audits of all types of processes will become more common. The most effective companies will establish programs of ongoing audits, whereby a number of goals can be accomplished:

- Performance improvements can be measured over time.

- Important changes in the company's environment can be systematically monitored.

- Managers can make a habit of change and improvement, rather than resisting it.

- Those areas that are of highest importance to the company can be routinely improved.

- Processes can be modified to be in alignment with changes in strategy or in the environment.

As with all management techniques, however, an enduring program of ongoing audits requires that audits become integrated into the overall management system. The following guidelines are keys to weaving audits into the fabric of day-to-day operations.

Establish Support for Ongoing Audits

While support for audits begins at the executive level, ownership for the audit process must be felt throughout the organization if an ongoing program is to be successful. The following actions will help to broaden support for the audit process, while ensuring greater benefit from the audit.

- *Share the results of the audit with everyone throughout the organization.*

By keeping others informed about the results of an audit, managers reassure those who participate in and are affected by the audit of the integrity of the process. Employees sometimes become suspicious of probing investigators; they may have doubts about how the information will be used, or whether the information will be used. By sharing audit results, managers make an implicit commitment to improving the processes that have been evaluated.

• *Act on the audit results.*

Questions will be raised about continuing audits if early assessments bear no fruits. Failing to act on performance gaps that are identified leads to cynicism and lack of trust among those who work with the problems daily. On the other hand, improving a process can create the momentum that comes from accomplishment. Committing resources and attention to the improvement opportunities revealed by an audit also shows management commitment to the improvement process.

• *Let others know when performance has improved.*

Communicating the positive results from an audit is one way of rewarding the people who contributed to that improvement. It also builds faith in the effectiveness of the audit process. Moreover, showing that performance has improved is another means of reassuring people of a commitment to the improvement process.

• *Reward people for their part in improvements.*

Increasing efficiency and effectiveness can often be a threatening experience for those who are involved in a work process. Improving the way resources are used often means eliminating the need for some of the people who have been involved in the process. Although flatter, leaner organizations often preclude the possibility of offering promotions, managers should nevertheless attempt to ensure that people who contribute to performance improvement find their own situations better rather than worse as a result.

Rewards for helping to close performance gaps may span a range from thanking people for their efforts to planning a group celebration to offering bonuses or pay increases for improvement. Rewards are especially meaningful when people are allowed to suggest what rewards they would like for their contribution. This may provide managers with new ideas for rewards that may be less costly to the organization than financial recognition.

• *Involve a wide variety of people in the audit process.*

People can be involved in the audit process in many ways. By involving people from a broad spectrum, more people learn about audit techniques and results, thus spreading commitment to the audit process throughout the organization. By involving many people in the data-gathering process, employees feel that action plans growing out of the audit were a result of their input. Excluding people from the data-gathering phase usually reduces the feeling of ownership for the results, thus making people feel as if initiatives are being imposed on them. By the same token, involving a broad range of people in the development of action plans expands ownership for the plans and allows for the generation of more ideas.

Part 5

IMPLEMENTING A BUSINESS STRATEGY AUDIT: QUESTIONS AND CHECKLISTS

This section of the Business Strategy Audit comprises a series of questions based on the three steps given in *Steps in Conducting an Environmental Assessment* (Part 1: The External Environment Assessment), the seven steps given in *Steps in Completing an Organizational Assessment* (Part 2: The Organizational Assessment), and the information given in Part 3: Integration and Implementation.

These questions have been designed to help you plan and implement your audit in a straightforward and practical manner, covering all the relevant parts of the audit in the correct sequence. Additionally, background information is given for each step before the questions themselves are listed.

Part 1 The External Environment Assessment
STEPS IN CONDUCTING AN ENVIRONMENTAL ASSESSMENT

- Step 1 Understand the Environment at a Macro Level
- Step 2 Understand the Industry Components in Detail
- Step 3 Integrate the Components into an Environmental Picture

Part 2 The Organizational Assessment
STEPS IN COMPLETING AN ORGANIZATIONAL ASSESSMENT

- Step 1 Clarify the Strategy
- Step 2 Measure Viability and Robustness
- Step 3 Outline Business Processes
- Step 4 Determine Capabilities
- Step 5 Determine Appropriate Organization Design & Resource Allocation
- Step 6 Assess the Company's Culture
- Step 7 Integrate the Elements of the Organization Assessment

Part 3 Integration and Implementation

Note: Steps 1, 2 and 3 in Part 1: The External Environment Assessment are best accomplished through study teams, as described in the main text under the subhead "Who Should Conduct the Assessment?" and visually in Figure 1.

UNDERSTAND THE ENVIRONMENT AT A MACRO LEVEL

BACKGROUND INFORMATION

The focus in Step 1, Part 1 is on the broader trends across and within industries. The first step in an environmental assessment is to develop a basic understanding of these trends along with other issues that will significantly change, influence and affect the industry.

The "Questions" section below will help you to arrive at an overall industry understanding by looking at the elements that influence the environment. They will also help with the issue of team staffing.

QUESTIONS

- In order to gain overall industry understanding, are you considering:
  - ❏ capital markets
  - ❏ industry capacity
  - ❏ technological factors
  - ❏ pressure from substitutes
  - ❏ threat of new entrants
  - ❏ economic factors
  - ❏ political factors
  - ❏ regulatory factors
  - ❏ geographical factors
  - ❏ social factors?

Now that you are aware of elements that influence the environment, you should examine the issue of team staffing.

- Will your leadership team comprise representative managers or leaders of different functions or groups within the company?

- Will additional people be added to ensure a wide range of:
  - ❏ backgrounds
  - ❏ talents
  - ❏ interests?

83

- In studying the environmental picture presented by the elements listed above, will the team include (from within the organization):
  - ❏ key technical players
  - ❏ natural leaders
  - ❏ idea leaders?

- In conducting the overview will it be taken into account that:
  - ❏ the environmental assessment should be considered from an external perspective
  - ❏ the assessment needs to be based on data (rather than intuitive insight)
  - ❏ managers may have a tendency to disregard negative information about the company and its products?

- Will the leadership team be honest and open about what is really happening in the environment?

Note: Information sources usually available for this part of the audit are listed in Figure 2, Step 1, Part 1.

- Has it been decided how the leadership team will gather the information after it has reviewed both what is needed and the suggested information sources?

A useful framework to understand these issues comes from answering the questions below. These questions are posed directly when used in the context of an interview, and used indirectly when analyzing data.

- What is the long-term viability of the industry as a whole, and how do capital markets react to new developments?

- What trends could change the rules of the game?

- Who are the industry leaders? What are they doing? Why?

- What are the key success factors in the industry?

- What developments could allow a company to change the rules of the game?

- Five years from now, how will winners in the industry look and act?

- What is the reward (and/or cost) of being a winner/loser within the industry?

- Where has the industry come from?

The questions for Step 1, Part 1 may have identified areas requiring further study. These areas can be explored below through the questions listed for Step 2, Part 1.

UNDERSTAND THE INDUSTRY COMPONENTS IN DETAIL

BACKGROUND INFORMATION

An in-depth look at the future and long-term viability of the industry can be undertaken by examining the following three components.

1   The company and its competitors.

2   Customers.

3   Other stakeholders.

The "Questions" section below begins by assessing the team tasks required for this part of the audit before going through each of these three components in turn.

QUESTIONS

Team Tasks

- Have the teams made preliminary findings and identified important issues from the review of the overall environment?

Note: These findings are the prerequisites for the study teams to begin their work.

- Will the teams studying the components of the environment use the set of industry analysis questions below to analyze where each group sees the industry heading?

- Will the teams studying the components of the environment address specific issues that are significant about the particular part of the industry assigned to them?

Industry analysis questions

- What is the long-term viability of the industry as a whole, and how do capital markets react to new developments?

- What trends could change the rules of the game?

- Who are the industry leaders? What are they doing? Why?

- What are the key success factors in the industry?

- What developments could allow a company to change the rules of the game?

- Five years from now, how will winners in the industry look and act?

- What is the reward (and/or cost) of being a winner/loser within the industry?

- Where has the industry come from?

Note: The teams that study the three components listed should understand the elements of both the overall strategy audit and the environmental assessment that their analysis will contribute to it.

1 The Company and its Competitors

- Will information gathered on competitors include that relating to the categories of:
  - ❏ A. business
  - ❏ B. financial
  - ❏ C. organization?

Below is a list of research questions that takes each of these categories into account.

A. *Business Review*

Strategy Issues:

- What is the strategy of each competitor? Where do they appear to be heading?

- What is their business emphasis?

- Do they compete on quality, cost, speed or service?

- Are they niche or global players?

Capabilities:

- What do they do better than anyone else?

- Where are they weaker than others?

- Where are they the same as others?

Business Objectives:

- Who are their primary customers?

- What types of business do they not do or say no to?

- Who are their major partners? Why are they partnering? What do they gain by partnering?

- What are they doing that is new or interesting?

B. *Financial Review*

Financial Strength — Internal:

- How much cash does each competitor generate annually?

- What are the drivers behind their financial success (from a cash perspective)?

- How do they allocate resources (funds)?

- How fast are they growing and in what areas?

Strength as Perceived by Capital Markets:

- Are competitors resource constrained or do they have strong financial backing?

- Is this perception consistent with the internal analysis? Why or why not?

- How has the company performed in the financial markets? Why?

- What constraints/opportunities do they have with respect to financial markets? Why?

C. *Organization Review*

Top Management:

- Has management kept the company at the forefront of the industry? Why or why not?

- Are the key players seen to be moving the company forward?

Organization:

- Is the company centralized or decentralized?

- Does the corporate parent act as a holding company or as an active manager?

- Is the organization perceived as being lean and able to get things done?

People:

- How many people are employed? Is the company over- or under-staffed?

- Are people managed to achieve mainly business objectives, human objectives or some of both? How does this affect the company?

- What skills are emphasized during recruitment?

Culture:

- Is the culture results-oriented?

- Bureaucratic?

- Flexible?

Having considered the information needed, the following questions will help to ascertain how it should be obtained, from whom, then how it should be analyzed.

- Will information relating to competitors be gathered from publicly available sources such as:
  - ❑ annual reports
  - ❑ investment presentations
  - ❑ journal articles
  - ❑ financial reports
  - ❑ internal and external reviews
  - ❑ interviews with customers
  - ❑ interviews with former employees or competitors
  - ❑ other published information?

- In terms of improving the quality of information gathered, will:
  - ❑ up-front analysis be undertaken on the available public data to identify key areas of focus
  - ❑ questions be asked in a way that does not require the interviewee to compromise his or her integrity?

- Will information be analyzed by sorting it into areas that:
  - ❑ reflect the current position of the competitors
  - ❑ project their future positioning?

Note: The information given in Figure 5, Step 2, Part 1 shows how information can usefully be divided into these two matrices.

- Can it be determined when sorting information whether any one competitor has a clear competitive advantage in the industry?

- Should the company be comparing this audit to others in the industry to provide an early indication of whether the company's processes support, or are aligned with, its strategy?

2. Customers

- Is the interface and relationship a company has with those who buy its products and those who use its services understood?

- Are managers aware of:
  - ❑ where the company does its business in the industry
  - ❑ the company's customers
  - ❑ the products bought by these customers
  - ❑ why customers choose to do business with the company rather than its competitors
  - ❑ the factors that will influence where customers will do business in the future?

- Will information gathered show:
  - ❑ an understanding of how customers affect the company
  - ❑ an understanding of how the company affects the customer and the customer's business?

- Will this understanding be framed in terms of:
  - ❑ where the company is today
  - ❑ where the company is likely to be in the future?

- In terms of understanding the customer's impact on the company, what does the company gain from working with a customer:
  - ❑ from a market or financial perspective
  - ❑ from a strategic or business perspective?

- Will a market or financial analysis seek to clarify the effect major customers have on the profitability of the company in terms of:
  - ❑ sales and sales growth trends
  - ❑ gross margin on products sold
  - ❑ "other costs" required to do business with the customer (cost to serve)?

Note: "Other costs" typically include: sales costs, delivery costs, customer service costs and administrative costs.

- Will the strategic or business perspective seek to clarify what the company does for the customer?

- Will the perspective seek to measure the intangible costs and benefits of doing business with them as well as assess the company's understanding of how well it knows its customers' needs?

In order to study the strategic and business perspective more fully, the following four questions also need to be answered. These four questions should also be asked both in terms of where the company is today, and where managers see the business going.

- Does the business we do with this customer provide us with competitive advantage that is transferable to other customers?

- What resources are we giving up by working with this customer that we could use to service other customers?

- Why do we think the customers buys from us?

- What do we provide for the customer that others do not provide?

The next two sets of questions relate to understanding the company's impact on the customer or customer's business. The first set relates to commercial customers; the second relates to the individual consumer.

Commercial Customers

- Is the customer's environment (or industry) understood at a macro level?

Note: This includes investigating the same topics that were covered in the macro-level assessment for the company. See Step 1, Part 1.

- Is the customer's business and place in the industry understood?

Note: The information and data necessary to complete the analysis falls under the same three categories as it did for the competitor analysis. See Figure 4, Step 2, Part 1.

- Is it understood how the company fits into:
  - ❏ what the customer does
  - ❏ what part it plays in determining where the customer is in the industry today
  - ❏ where it is heading in the industry?

- Is it understood that this analysis should be done at:
  - ❏ a broad strategic level
  - ❏ an operational level
  - ❏ an ease-of-doing-business level?

- Will analysis at the broad strategic level involve determining how the company adds value to its customer's business from:
  - ❏ an economic perspective
  - ❏ a strategic perspective?

- In order to reveal why customers buy from the company rather than from its competitors, will analysis at an operational level look at the buyer–purchase criteria?

Buyer–purchase criteria analysis is done by answering the following five questions.

- Why do customers buy from us instead of from others?

- What factors influence buying decisions and what is the relative importance of these factors?

- What do customers look at when comparing products?

- Who usually gets the sale?

- Why?

Note: The purpose of buyer–purchase criteria analysis is to understand the most important buying factors (such as cost, quality, service or innovation) from the customer's perspective.

- Will analysis of the ease-of-doing-business level include issues such as:
  - ❏ billing
  - ❏ customer service

- ❑ order processing
- ❑ communications
- ❑ others?

Note: Understanding these factors will help to assess whether the company is attending to them in such a way that it does not create competitive disadvantage.

Individual Consumers

- Will insight into how the company's products affect the customer be given by undertaking a review of:
  - ❑ trends
  - ❑ customer preferences
  - ❑ buying patterns
  - ❑ social factors
  - ❑ others?

Note: Much of this research may already have been done by market research staff, or may be available commercially.

Having considered the information needed, the following questions will help to ascertain how it should be obtained, from whom, then how it should be analyzed.

- Will customer analysis include a broad sampling of customers for different products?

- Will these samples include one or two lead customers or customer groups responsible for the majority of sales for each product?

- Will a range of different types of customer be talked to, including:
  - ❑ new customers
  - ❑ customers in different industries
  - ❑ customers who put the product to different end uses
  - ❑ past customers who have recently switched to another supplier
  - ❑ other customers?

Note: The best source of information varies for each segment of the customer analysis, as outlined under the subhead "How is the information obtained and from whom?" which is part of "2. CUSTOMERS" in Step 2, Part 1.

- Will the data gathered about customers be examined in terms of:
  - ❏ today and the future
  - ❏ the importance to the company
  - ❏ the importance to the customer
  - ❏ the customer's perspective
  - ❏ the company's perspective?

- Does the company need to create distinctiveness with the customer?

- How will the company create distinctiveness with the customer?

3. Other Stakeholders

- Do stakeholders of the company include:
  - ❏ suppliers
  - ❏ regulatory agencies
  - ❏ public interest groups
  - ❏ stock holders
  - ❏ others?

Note: Stakeholders are those beyond a company's customers and competitors who affect or are affected by the company and its operations.

- Will the analysis determine the expectations and viewpoints of stakeholders with respect to the company?

In order to gather relevant information, stakeholders themselves will need to be asked the following seven questions.

- What does the stakeholder need from the company?

- What does the stakeholder value about the company?

- What is the stakeholder's role in relation to the business?

- What do they expect of the company?

- What are some potential roadblocks for the company as it pursues its business objectives?

- What opportunities should the company pursue that differ from what it is doing today?

- Does the stakeholder have a viewpoint about what the company can do to achieve competitive advantage in the marketplace?

Note: Viewpoints expressed by stakeholders often differ substantially from what customers say or what industry analysts foresee.

Having considered the information needed, the following questions will help to ascertain how it should be obtained, from whom, then how it should be analyzed.

- Has the company understood stakeholders who are:
  - ❑ shareholders
  - ❑ end users
  - ❑ environmental groups
  - ❑ politicians/public policy experts
  - ❑ regulatory agencies
  - ❑ joint venture partners
  - ❑ technologists
  - ❑ corporate holding companies?

- Will interviews be conducted with:
  - ❑ representatives from each of the above stakeholder groups
  - ❑ others who understand the perspectives of various stakeholders?

- Will interview responses from stakeholders be grouped into those that are:
  - ❑ expectations
  - ❑ opportunities
  - ❑ threats?

Having answered all the questions in this sizeable section on understanding the industry components in detail, the questions below relating to Step 3, Part 1 will help you to integrate the components into an environmental picture.

Integrate the Components into an Environmental Picture

BACKGROUND INFORMATION

Integrating different components of analysis data should take place at two levels.

1 Assessing where the industry is heading and the likely impact of that direction on the company.

2 Combining the organizational assessment with the environmental assessment.

The questions below will help you to use a suitable framework for integrating your data.

QUESTIONS

- Have you drawn up a framework in order to analyze the information you have gathered?

Your framework should include the following questions.

- What is the viability of the industry?

- What developments could change the rules of the game?

- What are the industry leaders doing? Why?

- What are the key success factors in the industry?

- What will winners look like five years from now?

- Where is the industry heading?

- Which competitors are positioning themselves for industry leadership in the future?

- What capabilities do they have?

- What do customers want in the future?

Note: An industry analysis framework is shown in Figure 6, Step 3, Part 1.

- Will your analysis highlight significant changes in the environment?

- Will your analysis highlight the impact of those changes on the company's competitive position with the industry?

- Will your analysis highlight the fundamental question of how the company can influence its environment in the future?

- Will your analysis highlight what the business will need to look like if it is to thrive in the future?

- Will your analysis highlight the requirements and capabilities that are needed by the company to meet external demands?

- Will these requirements and needs be matched up with the current capabilities outlined in the organization assessment?

Having examined and analyzed the company's environment by answering all of the questions in Part 1, managers should now consider the qualities and characteristics of the organization itself that influence what can be accomplished in terms of strategy. Part 2 poses some questions that will help you to make an organizational assessment.

Step **1**

CLARIFY THE STRATEGY

Note: Before you answer the questions for each of the seven steps in Part 2, it is important to study Figure 7 in the section headed *Steps in Completing an Organizational Assessment*, which gives a visual and detailed overview of the organizational assessment. It will also help if you refer to the text in the same section.

BACKGROUND INFORMATION

Strategy clarification determines the following four things.

1 A description of the business.

2 A description of the strategy.

3 How the firm is distinct or how it gains advantage.

4 The clarity of the strategy throughout the organization.

In the "Questions" section below you will find a set of questions for each of these four areas.

QUESTIONS

1 A Description of the Business

- Will a description of the business include information about:
  - ❏ what industry the company is in
  - ❏ what niche(s) the company competes in
  - ❏ what part of the industry management has decided to focus on
  - ❏ the strategic objectives of the business
  - ❏ the mission, vision, and values of the firm?

- Will the management describe or provide written documentation about each of the above areas?

- Will the study team try to determine if the stated goals of the business depict what actually happens in day-to-day operations?

- If a discrepancy exists, will it be noted for future design?

Note: Discrepancies are usually a sign of misaligned support systems or miscommunication.

- If the strategy is not clear, or if managers want to change the company's strategy, will the leadership team examine its own beliefs and assumptions, along with beliefs and assumptions that are held industry-wide, about how competitive advantage is gained?

Note: If traditional ways of doing things are limiting a company's performance, then challenging either industry or organizational beliefs and assumptions by doing business differently can lead to competitive advantage.

2 A Description of the Strategy

- As well as describing what business an organization is in, will the leadership team also describe what strategy the company is pursuing in that business?

- Will team members want to review presentations that have been made to investors where strategy has been described?

- Will team members want to look at decisions that have been made historically?

- Which products or markets has the organization withdrawn from, especially when getting out of a market has affected the company's direction?

- How clear is the strategy in the minds of people throughout the organization?

- Have strategies been dismissed because the company appears to have little focus?

- Might this lack of focus be due to problems in the company's communication process or in the organization's design rather than the strategy itself?

- To determine where any problems are, will the team ask employees (and those in charge of implementing the strategy):
  - ❑ how they interpret and describe the company's strategy
  - ❑ what problems they see with the strategy
  - ❑ how what they are asked to produce compares with what they are rewarded for?

Note: Answers to the above question may provide significant insights into what the company's actual strategy is, how well it is being communicated, and how people on the front lines think that it could be improved.

3 How the Firm is Distinct or How it Gains Advantage

- Has the organization made a specific effort to determine how to prioritize initiatives and commitment of resources in order to avoid becoming unfocused or producing a mediocre performance?

- Does the organization spend all of its resources and time trying to do everything well, and thus end up being viewed as having nothing different, unique, or better in comparison to other players in the market?

- Do customers have compelling reasons to develop a loyalty relationship with the company?

4 The Clarity of the Strategy Throughout the Organization

- Are audit teams aware of the sources available to them to help them find the data they need?

Note: These sources are listed in Figure 8, Step 1, Part 2.

- Has a list of questions been prepared to ask of:
  - ❏ experts
  - ❏ in-house specialists
  - ❏ planning group members?

Below is a list of questions that could be asked in strategy clarification.

- What (if anything) gives this business distinctiveness?

- What skills does this business currently have that are better than those of the competition? Can this advantage be sustained for a period of more than a few years?

- How is this company generally regarded in the industry or by outside experts? How do outsiders see the company's strategy? What do they think about it?

- What are this company's strengths in creating a world-class organization?

- What are the biggest roadblocks to this business becoming a world class organization?

- What does the company do? Why?
  What does it not do? Why not?

Who are its customers? Who are not its customers?
What are its products? What are not its products?
What are its markets? What are not its markets?

- Why is the company in this business and not another?

- Why is the company focusing on these customers and not others? Why is it making these products (or providing these services) and not others?

- What direction do the company's vision, mission, and strategic objectives statements suggest?

- Does this business have more than one strategy?

Note: The questions to ask in strategy clarification can also be used as questions to guide research in reports and periodicals.

- Has the audit team determined what kind of information is needed to best complete the strategy audit?

Note: The team could use all or few of these sources, depending on the objectives of the audit, and the time and resources available.

Once strategy has been clarified, viability and robustness testing will help audit teams to determine current performance and future industry requirements. Answering the questions that relate to Step 2, Part 2, will help to measure viability and robustness in your company.

MEASURE VIABILITY AND ROBUSTNESS

BACKGROUND INFORMATION

Having key measures about current performance and future requirements in place ensures implementation and proper feedback of vital data necessary to make adjustments to strategy or tactics. Step 2, Part 2 therefore looks at the following.

1. Current performance and viability.

2. Future performance and viability.

Answering the questions below will help you to measure viability and robustness within your own company, both now and in the future.

QUESTIONS

1 Current Performance and Viability

- Is the organization meeting its strategic objectives?

- What areas in the business have exceeded expectations?

- Why?

- Which areas need improvement?

- How does the performance of the business compare to that of competitors?

- How does the company's current performance compare to its past performance?

Note: Helpful sources of information include figures describing the company's market share, success rates, cycle time, or other ratios specific to the business. This information can be found in annual reports, industry reports, internal financial statements, marketing analysis and so on.

2 Future Performance and Viability

- In order to determine robustness, will the leadership team brainstorm different scenarios that describe possible changes in the future business environment?

- Will the leadership team brainstorm contrasting scenarios such as:
  - ❏ price increases
  - ❏ price decreases
  - ❏ retail domination
  - ❏ wholesale domination
  - ❏ constrained resources
  - ❏ increased government regulation
  - ❏ increased international competition and the opening or collapse of world markets?

Note: The purpose of the brainstorms is to develop four or five unique scenarios that describe possible changes in the business environment.

- For each scenario generated, will the business strategy be tested for its market viability?

- In testing the business strategy, will the audit team ask questions such as:
  - ❏ "Will competitive density increase or decrease?"
  - ❏ "Will our capture rate increase or decrease?"
  - ❏ "Will this strategy make us distinct?"
  - ❏ "Will this strategy provide customers with what they want?"?

- Will future financial viability be determined by looking at returns received on the money required to do business?

To help determine future financial viability, the team should ask the following four questions.

- In order to increase these returns, what must be done?

- What are the factors that influence the return on investment?

- Which factors need to be emphasized or improved?

- In which scenario will this strategy lead to more sales, lower costs, higher profits, lower entry costs, or decreased lead time?

Note: There may be other measures more specific to a given business that the audit team should examine and monitor in the future in order to ensure alignment with the direction of the business.

The questions that follow are additional questions to be asked by the audit team in assessing viability and robustness.

- Does this strategy give us the market share we need and expect?

- What kind of demand is there for this product or service?

- Will this strategy provide sustainable competitive advantage?

- Will this strategy help us accomplish our strategic objectives?

- What kind of future opportunity is there if this strategy is followed?

- What are the vulnerabilities of this strategy?

- Is this strategy consistent with the environment and changing customer needs?

- What value does this give our shareholders?

- How does this strategy fare in future mapping or scenario analysis?

- How easily and quickly can this strategy be copied?

Having ascertained how viability and robustness can be measured in your company, the next step in the business strategy audit is to outline your business processes. The questions below, which relate to Step 3, Part 2, will help you to do this.

OUTLINE BUSINESS PROCESSES

BACKGROUND INFORMATION

There are certain processes in every business that must exist in order to deliver products and services to the customer, either internal or external. These processes are examined through the following.

1 Macro work flow.

2 Process analysis and improvement.

3 Process improvement through best practices analysis.

In the "Questions" section below you will find a set of questions relating to each of these.

QUESTIONS

1 Macro Work Flow

- Will the audit team construct a macro work flow for delivering products or services to the customer?

- Will the macro work flow include everything from the initial conceptualization of a product all the way through to sales and services?

Note: Two hypothetical examples of macro work flows are shown in Figure 11, Step 3, Part 2.

- Will the strategy define:
  - ❏ how the business gains distinctiveness in the eyes of customers
  - ❏ what is different about the relationship the business will have with its customers versus the relationship competitors have with customers
  - ❏ what must be emphasized to gain competitive advantage?

- After the team has determined the macro work flow, will it determine what part of that work flow should be emphasized, given the strategy?

2 Process Analysis and Improvement

- Will the team decide first which processes are core to the business and which are support work?

Note: The processes in the macro work flows can be divided into four categories, as outlined under the subhead "Process Analysis and Improvement" in Step 3, Part 2.

- Will managers then concentrate on improving the core processes to a performance level that exceeds that of competitors?

- Will managers be very clear about what is support work to the business and perform that work at parity with the competition?

- Will the level of capability required in core work and support work be looked at carefully?

3 Process Improvement Through Best Practices Analysis

- Before adopting best practices, will managers consider:
  - ❏ whether it would dilute or leverage resources
  - ❏ whether it is core to the business
  - ❏ whether it leverages the unit of competitive advantage
  - ❏ whether other companies provide the service to the client more effectively at a lower cost?

The next step in the audit process is to determine the capabilities required and whether or not they are currently available. The questions below, which relate to Step 4, Part 2, will help to ascertain this.

DETERMINE CAPABILITIES

BACKGROUND INFORMATION

There are two elements central to determining capabilities.

1 Knowing what the required capabilities are.

2 Knowing whether the business has the necessary skills and capabilities to successfully execute the chosen strategy.

Answering the questions below will help you to gather the information you require.

QUESTIONS

- Once core processes have been outlined, will capabilities need to be improved to a level that exceeds the performance of competitors in those processes and gives a business distinctiveness?

- Will support work, which is outside the core processes, be improved only to parity with competition?

- Will the processes that give customers the products and services they most want be looked at?

Note: This can be done by reviewing the process analysis completed earlier.

- Will managers decide what must be done to deliver those products at:
  - ❏ lower cost
  - ❏ better quality
  - ❏ superior service
  - ❏ improved speed?

Note: The answers to the question above will indicate the capabilities required.

- Can the level of capability an organization has in these core processes be determined?

- Will this be done by talking to a variety of people that are involved with the business, such as:

  ❏ employees

  ❏ suppliers

  ❏ customers?

Note: Internal and external sources that can be helpful in determining capabilities are shown in Figure 12, Step 4, Part 2.

Below is a list of questions that can be used for your capability analysis when talking to people involved with the business.

- What is this business really good at?

- What skills does this business currently have that are better than those of competitors?

- What capabilities are needed with this strategy? (This should be answered by looking at the key processes that create competitive advantage.)

- Where do customers say we need to improve?

- What is the gap between current capabilities and capabilities needed to give the company advantage?

- How easy is it to acquire or build the needed capabilities?

- How much time and money will be needed to develop these skills?

- What is the organizational impact of this skills transition?

- Why have projects been lost and to whom were they lost?

- Where and how is the competition beating the company?

- What specific skills are contained within the capability bundles?

- How are these capability bundles arranged to gain competitive advantage?

- What programs does the company need or have in place that are designed to improve capabilities?

Note: Team members asking these questions should be careful about how much weight is given to each response. Interviewers should gather enough data from different perspectives to test the validity of what various respondents say – both positive and negative comments.

- Will a plan be developed that will improve or acquire the capabilities required?

- Will Human Resource personnel help identify what programs are currently in place?

Note: The need for assessing capabilities is shown in Figure 14, Step 4, Part 2.

Steps 1 to 4 of Part 2 will have provided audit teams with much data. The questions in Step 5, Part 2 will help to determine how an organization should implement these audit results.

DETERMINE APPROPRIATE ORGANIZATION DESIGN AND RESOURCE ALLOCATION

BACKGROUND INFORMATION

Evaluating organization design and resource allocation bridges the gap between data-gathering and strategy implementation. The most critical element of organization design is alignment. Step 5, Part 2 makes a study of the following.

1 Alignment.

2 Gathering alignment data.

3 Organizational structure.

4 Resourcing decisions.

The questions that follow cover each of these in turn.

QUESTIONS

1 Alignment

- Will the audit team evaluate the organization's design in terms of its ability to align internal rewards, support systems, feedback loops, etc., with the strategy of the business?

Note: Some common misalignments are shown in Figure 15, Step 5, Part 2. A definition of each of the elements within the models can be seen in Figure 16.

2 Gathering Alignment Data

- Will the leadership team find misalignments and recommend organizational design changes that ensure continued alignment?

- Will it be determined how well the organization is aligned with its strategy and environment through:

  ❏ focus groups

  ❏ surveys

  ❏ interviews with managers and employees within the organization?

- Is it understood that the goals of conducting focus groups, sending out surveys, and interviewing employees are to:
    - ❏ understand the employees' perception of the current strategy
    - ❏ identify areas of current organizational misalignment
    - ❏ identify key issues or barriers related to the successful implementation of the strategy?

The questions that follow could be used in conducting focus groups and interviews to assess organizational design needs.

- What is your view of the current organizational strategy?

- What parts of the organization are well-aligned to deliver the strategy?

- What current beliefs, policies, procedures, systems, or any other examples of misalignment do you see?

- What strategic initiatives are going well?

- What are the things that get in the way of the organization implementing its strategy? (This may include structure, boundary issues, reward systems, capabilities, processes, information, etc.)

- What are the things in the organization that are working well to support the implementation of the strategy?

- What does the organization need to do better to execute the strategy effectively?

- What gets in the way of people doing their work? Are there areas where effort is wasted?

- How do people spend their time?

- Where should efforts be focused to ensure competitive advantage?

- What are the opportunity areas for improving efficiency and effectiveness?

Note: A sample survey for gathering alignment data is given in Figure 18, Step 4, Part 2.

3 Organizational Structure

- Will the audit team revisit the macro work flow developed earlier to determine how the work actually occurs within those processes?

Note: Macro work flow was covered in Step 3, Part 2.

- Will the team study:
  - ❏ the sequence in which work occurs
  - ❏ where the key problems in the process lie
  - ❏ where the interdependencies occur in the process
  - ❏ which organizational units perform each piece of the work?

Note: The answers to the question above will help determine whether the current structure helps or hinders hand-offs, interdependencies, and the accomplishment of work.

4 Resourcing Decisions

- Does the company need to own all of its support processes, or can some of them be contracted out?

Note: Figure 19, Step 5, Part 2 provides a decision tool about whether or not processes should be owned, or whether the work can be contracted out to others.

- Will contracting out work allow managers to focus resources on improving the source of the company's competitive advantage?

- Will contracting out work allow access to superior products and services offered by firms that make those offerings their core work?

Once these questions have been answered, it's time to move on to assessing the company's culture. The questions that relate to Step 6, Part 2 will help you to do this.

ASSESS THE COMPANY'S CULTURE

BACKGROUND INFORMATION

Culture consists of values, beliefs, and norms that manifest themselves in the habitual ways organization members accomplish their work, relate to one another, and solve problems that confront them. Understanding a company's culture helps decision makers understand:

- why choices have been made in the past
- the ability and willingness of the organization to change
- the roadblocks to strategy implementation.

The questions that follow will help you to assess your company's culture.

QUESTIONS

- As the audit team completes its organizational assessment, will it pay constant attention to the culture?

- Will the audit team ask:
  - ❏ why things are done the way they are
  - ❏ whether the culture is changing in any way?

- Will the assessment uncover the basic beliefs and assumptions that are widely shared in an organization?

- Will the assessment construct a picture of how the organization operates?

- Will the leadership style, company history, and organizational beliefs and assumptions be analysed and understood before attempting to change a company's strategy?

- If changes in the strategy or organization are required, will the elements of culture listed in the question above contribute or detract from the strategy implementation?

- Will audit teams pay special attention to these elements of culture to ensure:
  - ❏ alignment
  - ❏ change in the organization
  - ❏ successful implementation of strategic objectives?

Having assessed the company's culture, the final step in this business strategy audit is to construct a framework that provides a systematic way of summarizing the findings of the organization assessment.

INTEGRATE THE ELEMENTS OF THE ORGANIZATION ASSESSMENT

BACKGROUND INFORMATION

A framework structure should be used to determine what organizational factors should be considered in strategy implementation. The framework shown in Figure 20, Step 7, Part 2 provides a systematic approach.

The questions that follow should all be used within your framework for industry analysis.

QUESTIONS

- What is our strategy?

- How has it changed in the past five years?

- How is it likely to change in the future?

- How viable and robust is our business?

- How does our current strategy hold up under various future scenarios?

- What measures determine viability and robustness?

- What are our major business processes?

- What aspects of those processes should be emphasized, given our strategy?

- What capabilities do we have now?

- Given our current strategy, what capabilities do we need to develop?

- What will it take to develop or acquire those capabilities?

- How well is our structure aligned with our strategy?

- Do our systems support our strategy?

- Are there systems that could be contracted out to others?

- Do your values and beliefs support the implementation of our strategy?

- How difficult will it be to accomplish the goals dictated by our strategy, given the way things are done in our company?

Note: The questions above should each be answered in terms of findings and impact.

The data gathering exercises that you will now have undertaken provide the tools for anticipating fundamental shifts in business environment, and what changes those shifts require from the organization. All that remains now is the task of integrating the findings. Part 3 provides a brief examination of this aspect of the audit.

INTEGRATION AND IMPLEMENTATION (PART 3)

BACKGROUND INFORMATION

As a strategy audit team completes the data gathering phases outlined in Parts 1 and 2, it needs to ask questions about the data's significance and validity. It should also consider the changes suggested by the data.

The question below will help to cover these important aspects.

QUESTION

- When making changes to the organization, will managers consider that:
  - ❏ structure follows strategy
  - ❏ plans for change must be widely owned
  - ❏ implementation should start with what is core to gaining advantage
  - ❏ certain common mistakes will need to be avoided?

Note: A list of common mistakes is given under the bullet point "Avoid the following mistakes" in Part 3 of this audit.

IN CONCLUSION ...

All of the questions listed in this part of the business strategy audit will hopefully help you to plan an audit that will help your organization to understand the strategy, what leads to competitive advantage, and where time and attention should be focused. The extensive explanations in Parts 1, 2 and 3 will help you to answer these questions to best effect.

Good luck!

SUMMARY

Today's industries are changing at incredible speeds. Technology is advancing and changing customers' expectations and the way companies compete. Changing equally as fast are the number of books and articles that explain new and innovative ideas about how to deal with changing environmental conditions. While many of these ideas are helpful, they can be distractions that drain resources and provide little benefit if they are adopted without a clear understanding of the business environment and the strategy an organization has chosen to pursue. If everyone in the organization understands the strategy, what leads to competitive advantage, and where time and attention should be focused, these new management ideas can be prioritized in a way that ensures successful strategy implementation even in fast-changing environmental conditions.

Parts 1, 2 and 3: **Vernal Della-Piana, Murray Low** *and* **Kendall Lyman** *are consultants with Novations Group, Inc., in Provo, Utah, USA. They specialize in helping companies to clarify, implement, and align strategy. Their recent client list includes Amoco, Mobil, Scott Paper, and Hallmark.* **Part 4** *has been adapted from* The Company AuditGuide *published by Cambridge Strategy Publications Ltd.* **Part 5** *has been developed by Cambridge Strategy Publications Ltd.*